Social-Emotional Learning Activities

For Middle School

Contributing Authors

**Terri Akin • David Cowan • Gerry Dunne
Susanna Palomares • Dianne Schilling**

INNERCHOICE Publishing

Copyright © 2022, INNERCHOICE PUBLISHING • All rights reserved

    ISBN-10: 1-56499-103-2

    ISBN-13: 978-1-56499-103-4

Student experience sheets may be reproduced in quantities sufficient for distribution to students in groups utilizing *Social-Emotional Learning Activities for Middle School*. All other reproduction for any purpose whatsoever is explicitly prohibited without written permission. Requests for permission may be directed to INNERCHOICE PUBLISHING.

15079 Oak Chase Court
Wellington, FL 33414

www.InnerchoicePublishing.com

Contents

Introduction 1

The Impact of Social and Emotional Learning 3

Sharing Circles: The SEL Super Strategy 9

How to Conduct Sharing Circles 11

Self-Awareness 15

Self-Management 39

Social Awareness 79

Relationship Skills 111

Responsible Decision Making 151

Introduction

This activity guide is a collection of the most popular and effective social and emotional learning activities offered by Innerchoice Publishing. Over the years, Innerchoice Publishing has developed dozens of activity guides which have been used in thousands of schools throughout the country. Many of these books have been translated and used sucessfully in other countries interested in developing the emotional and social aspects of students lives. You are invited to use this newest contribution to the SEL curricular mosaic as:

- the core of your SEL curriculum
- a specialized SEL supplement to your existing curriculum

This book provides relevant student friendly activities for classroom and counseling groups. For optimum impact SEL is not a single program or group of activities but a coordinated framework across classrooms, counseling groups, homes, communities and districts.

The bottom line is, don't neglect or take for granted the emotional life of your students. Feelings, self-awareness, life skills, conflict management, self-esteem, and all of the other developmental areas now identified as social emotional learning are critically important. An impressive array of research from multiple fields supports the validity of time and energy spent by educators in these domains. Emotions are not unruly remnants of stone-age survival to be hushed and otherwise ignored while we develop cognitive skills. Emotions drive our behavior, shape our values, and predispose us to choose one course of action over others. Emotional and rational skills are equally important interdependent components of human intelligence.

Unit Organization

The five units in this guide each contain group activities, Sharing Circles, individual experience sheets, and comprise a complete SEL curriculum. The Collaborative for Academic, Social, and Emotional Learning (CASEL) has identified five core social and emotional competencies: Self-awarenwss, Self-management, Social Awareness, Relationship Skills, and Responsible Decision Making. This book has utulized these competencies in it's chapter organization.

• Self-Awareness

Building a vocabulary for feelings, knowing the likes, dislikes, hopes, preferences, talents, shortcomings, and other uniquenesses that make up the individual. Becoming aware of inner and outer states and processes. Establishing a firm sense of identity and feeling esteem and acceptance of oneself; monitoring "self-talk" to catch negative messages such as internal put-downs; acknowledging the talents and abilities of self and others.

• Self-Management

Knowing the relationship between thoughts, feelings and actions; accurately reading feeling cues in others and responding appropriately; realizing what is behind feelings (e.g. the primary feelings underlying anger) and learning how to constructively express and control feelings. Understanding what stress is, where it comes from, and how it affects daily living; learning to use exercise, guided imagery, relaxation methods, and attitude changes to control and relieve stress.

• Social Awareness

Taking the perspective and understanding the feelings of others; developing caring and compassionate attitudes. Working self-reflectively in groups while monitoring behaviors and roles; practicing cooperation and interdependence.

• Relationship Skills

Learning and practicing effective communication skills; listening actively; and, engaging in effective two-way communication using good listening and speaking skills. Understanding that conflict is normal and potentially productive; learning how to fight fair with others; learning and practicing a variety of conflict-resolution strategies.

• Responsible Decision Making

Examining what goes into making decisions; considering actions and knowing their consequence; recognizing the existence of personal choice in almost all situations; taking responsibility for decisions and actions.

In addition to the group activities in each chapter there are six fully developed Sharing Circles. Before you lead your first Sharing Circle, be sure to read the section, "How to Conduct Sharing Circles" on page 11.

Many of the activities include handouts, called "Experience Sheets," for you to duplicate and distribute to students. Experience sheets are written in a conversational style and speak directly to the individual student. Directions for their use are imbedded in the printed procedure for leading each activity.

The units are arranged in a suggested order, but may be implemented with considerable flexibility. We encourage you to maintain an agile, expansive attitude as you move through (or skip among) the units. Allow the reactions of students to spark new ideas for strengthening social and emotional skills in each topic area.

Finally, please make any adjustments necessary to accommodate the interests, abilities, cultural backgrounds and learning styles of your students. Your experience and regular contact with students put you in an ideal position to interpret signals regarding relevancy and modify the activities accordingly.

The Impact of Social and Emotional Learning

Emotions impact every area of life: health, learning, behavior, and relationships.

Young people who are emotionally competent—who manage their own feelings well, and who recognize and respond effectively to the feelings of others — are at an advantage in every area of life, whether family and peer relationships, school, sports, or community and organizational pursuits. Students with well-developed emotional skills are also more likely to lead happy and productive lives, and to master the habits of mind that will assure them personal and career success as adults.

In homes and schools where social and emotional learning is nurtured, students tolerate frustration better, get into fewer fights, and engage in less self-destructive behavior. They are healthier, less lonely, less impulsive, and more focused. Human relationships improve, and so does academic achievement.

Health

There is no longer any question that emotions can profoundly affect health. Science used to believe that the brain and nervous system were separate and distinct from the immune system. In fact, the two systems are in close communication, sending messages back and forth continuously. Furthermore, chemical messengers which operate in both the brain and the immune system are concentrated *most heavily* in neural areas that regulate emotion.

Numerous studies have shown that positive, supportive relationships are good medicine, bolstering immune function, speeding recovery time, and prolonging life. The prognosis for people in ill health who have caring family and friends is dramatically better than for people without emotional support.

Learning

Almost all students who do poorly in school lack one or more elements of emotional intelligence. Study after study has shown that competence in emotional skills results not only in higher academic achievement on the part of students, but in significantly more instructional time on the part of teachers. Emotionally competent students are far less disruptive and require fewer disciplinary interventions.

Research has shown impressive benefits for students who participate in SEL programs. A meta-analysis published in the journal Child Development showed an 11 percentile gain in academic achievement. A study published in the Journal of Benefit-Cost Analysis, conducted by economist Clive Belfield and colleagues at Teachers College, Columbia University, demonstrated a roughly $11 benefit for every $1 spent on rigorous SEL programing.

Students who are emotionally competent have an increased desire to learn and to achieve, both within school and without. Positive emotions — excitement, curiosity, pride — are the fuel that drives motivation. Passion moves young people toward their goals.

Behavior

Violence and disorder in America's schools have reached crisis proportions. Teachers who once dealt with mischievous, unruly students and an occasional temper tantrum are now demanding emergency phones in their classrooms, security guards in the hallways, and metal detectors at the gates. As long as such conditions continue, all education suffers. Rates of teen suicide, pregnancy, and drug abuse testify to the need for emotional literacy: self-awareness, decision-making, self-confidence, and stress management.

Relationships

Students who are effective in social interactions are capable of understanding their peers. They know how to interact with other students and adults — flexibly, skillfully, and responsibly — without sacrificing their own needs and integrity. They have a good sense of timing and are effective at being heard and getting help when they need it. Socially competent students can process the nonverbal as well as verbal messages of others, and recognize that the behaviors of one person can affect another. They take responsibility for their actions.

Students who cannot interpret or express emotions feel frustrated. They don't understand what's going on around them. They are frequently viewed as strange, and cause others to feel uncomfortable. Without social competence, students can easily misinterpret a look or statement and respond inappropriately, yet lack the ability to express their uncertainty or clarify the intentions and desires of others. They may lack empathy and be relatively unaware of how their behavior affects others.

Controlling Emotions

The ability to bring out-of-control emotions back into line results in what our parents and grandparents called emotional maturity. Present terminology labels it emotional competence, or self-management the "master aptitude."

Self-Awareness

The first step in getting students to control their emotional responses is to help them develop self-awareness. Through self-awareness, students learn to give ongoing attention to their internal states, to know what they are feeling when they are feeling it, to identify the events that precipitate upsets and emotional hijackings, and to bring their feelings back under control.

Self-awareness allows students to manage their feelings and to recover from bad moods more quickly. Students who are self-aware don't hide things from themselves. Labeling feelings makes them their own. They can talk about fear, frustration, excitement, and envy and they can understand and speculate concerning such feelings in others, too.

Lacking self-awareness, students may become engulfed by their feelings, lost in them, overwhelmed by them. Unawareness of what is going on in their inner and outer worlds sets the stage for lack of congruence between what they believe or feel and how they behave. Feelings of isolation ("I'm the only one who feels this way.") occur when students are unaware that others experience the same range of feelings that they do. Without self-awareness students never gain control over their lives. By default, their courses are plotted by others or by parts of themselves which they fail to recognize.

Self-awareness can take the form of nonjudgmental observation ("I'm feeling irritated.") or it can be accompanied by evaluative thoughts ("I shouldn't feel this way" or "Don't think about that.") Although in and of themselves, emotions are neither right nor wrong, good nor bad, these kinds of judgments are common and indicate that the neocortical circuits are monitoring the emotion. However, to try to abolish a feeling or attempt to take away a feeling in someone else only drives the emotion out of awareness, where its activity along neural pathways continues unmonitored and unabated — as neuroses, insomnia, ulcers, and communication failures of all kinds testify.

Managing Anger and Curbing Impulses

Contrary to what many of us used to believe, when it comes to anger "letting it all out" is *not* helpful. Acting on anger will generally make a person angrier, and each angry outburst will prolong and deepen the distress.

What does work is to teach students to keep a lid on their feelings while they buy some time. If students wait until they have cooled down, they can confront the other person calmly. When flooded with negative emotions the ability to hear, think, and speak are severely impaired. Taking a "time out" can be enormously constructive. However 5 minutes is not enough; research suggests that people need at least 20 minutes to recover from intense physiological arousal.

Research has also shown quite conclusively that it's possible for a person to keep an angry mood going (and growing) just by thinking (and talking) about it.

The longer a student dwells on what made them angry, the more reasons and self-justifications can be found for being angry. So when encouraging students to talk about their feelings, we need to be careful not to fan the flames.

Brooding fuels anger, but seeing things differently quells it. Reframing a situation is one of the most potent ways of controlling emotions.

Sadness: Shifting Gears

Depression and sadness are low-arousal states. When a person is sad, it's as though a master gauge has turned down everything: mouth, eyes, head, shoulders, speech, energy, motivation, desire. Taking a jog is probably the last thing anyone feels like doing, but by forcing oneself out the door and down the path, a lift will beexperienced.

The key seems to be shifting the mind from a low-arousal state to a high-arousal state. Exercise and positive distracting activities, like seeing a funny movie, turn up the master gauge, relieving sadness, melancholy, and mild depression. Another way to accomplish the shift is to engineer a small success, such as improving a skill, winning a game, or completing a project.

Humor is great at lifting students out of the doldrums and can add significantly to their creativity and ability to solve problems, too. In studies documenting the effects of humor, people were able to think more broadly, associate more freely, and generate more creative solutions and decisions after hearing a joke.

The ability of humor to boost creativity and improve decision making stems from the fact that memory is "state specific." When we're in a good mood, we come up with more positive solutions and decisions. When we're in a bad mood, the alternatives we generate reflect our negativity.

Choosing to watch cartoons, shoot baskets, ride a bike, or spend a few minutes on the computer is a decision that the rational mind can take. The emotional mind can't be stopped from generating sadness and melancholy, but students can learn to tap into strategies that lead them out of the gloom.

Relationship Skills

If they are fortunate, students are surrounded by people who give them attention, are actively involved in their lives, and model healthy, responsible interpersonal behavior. Core skills in the art of relationships are empathy, listening, mastery of nonverbal cues, and the ability to manage the emotions of others — to make accurate interpretations, respond appropriately, work cooperatively, and resolve conflicts.

Howard Gardner's theory of multiple intelligence includes two personal intelligences, *interpersonal* and *intrapersonal*. People with high interpersonal intelligence have the capacity to discern and respond appropriately to the moods, temperaments, motivations, and desires of others. Intrapersonal intelligence gives people ready access to their own feeling life, the ability to discriminate among their emotions, and accurate awareness of their strengths and weaknesses.

The personal intelligences equip students to monitor their own expressions of emotion, attune to the ways others react, fine-tune their social performance to have the desired effect, express unspoken collective sentiments and guide groups toward goals. Personal intelligence is the basis of leadership.

Lacking personal intelligence, young people are apt to make poor choices related to such important decisions as who to befriend, emulate, date, and marry, what skills to develop and what career to pursue.

Empathy. All social skills are built on a base of emotional attunement, on the capacity for empathy. The ability to "walk in another's moccasins" is the foundation of caring and altruism. Violent people lack empathy.

Empathy is an outgrowth of self-awareness. The more we are able to understand our own emotions, the more skilled we are at understanding and responding to the emotions of others. Empathy plays heavily in making moral judgments. Sharing their pain, fear, or neglect is what moves us to help people in distress. Putting ourselves in the place of others motivates us to follow moral principles — to treat others the way we want to be treated.

These abilities have little to do with rational intelligence. Studies have shown that students with high levels of empathy are among the most popular, well adjusted, and high performing students, yet their IQs are no higher than those of students who are less skilled at reading nonverbal cues.

Empathy begins to develop very early in life. When infants and students under two witness the upset of another child, they react as if the distress were their own. Seeing another child cry is likely to bring them to tears and send them to a parent's arms.

From about the age of two on, when students begin to grasp the concept of their own separateness, they typically seek to console a distressed child by giving toys, petting, or hugging. In late childhood, they are able to view distress as an outgrowth of a person's condition or station in life. At this stage of development, students are capable of empathizing with entire groups such as the poor, the homeless, and victims of war.

Empathy can be developed through various forms of perspective-taking. In conflict situations, students can be asked to listen to each other's feelings and point of view, and then to feed back or summarize the opposing perspective. Imagining the feelings of characters in literature as well as figures from current events and history is also effective. Combining role playing with these strategies makes them even more powerful.

Nonverbal Communication Skills. The mode of communication used by the rational mind is words; the mode preferred by the emotional mind is nonverbal. We telegraph and receive excitement, happiness, sorrow, anger, and all the other emotions through facial expressions and body movements. When words contradict these nonverbal messages — "I'm fine," hissed through clenched teeth — nine times out of ten we can believe the nonverbal and discount the verbal.

Acting out various feelings teaches students to be more aware of nonverbal behavior, as does identifying feelings from videos, photos, and illustrations.

Emotions are contagious and transferrable. When two students interact, the more emotionally expressive of the pair readily transfers feelings to the more passive. Again, this transfer is accomplished *nonverbally*.

Students with high levels of emotional intelligence are able to attune to other students's (and adult's) moods and bring others under the sway of their own feelings, setting the emotional tone of an interaction.

Guided by cultural background, students learn certain display rules concerning the expression of emotions, such as minimizing or exaggerating particular feelings, or substituting one feeling for another, as when a child displays confidence while feeling confused. As educators in a multiethnic, multiracial society, we need to be sensitive to a variety of cultural display rules, and help students gain a similar awareness.

Listening. Through listening, students learn empathy, gather information, develop cooperative relationships, and build trust. Skillful listening is required for engaging in conversations and discussions, negotiating agreements, resolving conflicts and many other emotional and cognitive competencies.

Few skills have greater and more lasting value than listening. Unfortunately, listening skills are generally learned by happenstance, not by direct effort. The vast majority of students and adults are either unable or unwilling to listen attentively and at length to another person.

Research shows that poor listening impedes learning and destroys comprehension. However, when students are taught to listen effectively, both comprehension and academic performance go up, along with classroom cooperation and self-esteem. Listening facilitates both emotional learning and academic learning.

Conflict Management. Schools are rife with opportunities for conflict. From the farthest reaches of the campus to the most remote corners of the classroom, from student restrooms to the teacher's lounge, a thousand little things each day create discord. The causes are many.

Students bring to school an accumulation of everything they've learned — all of their habits and all the beliefs they've developed about themselves, other people, and their world. Such diversity makes conflict inevitable. And because the conflict-resolution skills of most students are poorly developed, the outcomes of conflict are frequently negative — at times even destructive.

Diversity also breeds conflict. Learning to understand, respect and appreciate similarities and differences is one key to resolving conflicts. Unfortunately most of us learn as students that there is only one right answer. From the moment this fallacious notion receives acceptance, the mind closes and vision narrows.

Prejudice cannot be eliminated, but the emotional learning underlying prejudice can be *relearned*. One way to accomplish relearning is to engineer projects and activities in which diverse groups work together to obtain common goals. Social cliques, particularly hostile ones, intensify negative stereotypes. But when students work together as equals to attain a common goal — on committees, sports teams, performing groups — stereotypes break down.

Educating the Emotional Brain

Social and Emotional skills are core competencies. To raise the level of these skills in students, schools need to focus more on the emotional aspects of students's lives, which are often ignored.

Unfortunately, in classes that stress subject-matter mastery, teaching is often devoid of emotional content. Too many educators believe that if somehow students master school subjects, they will be well prepared for life. Such a view suffers from a shallow and distorted understanding of how the human brain functions.

Many of the competencies that should be addressed by educational programs in SEL have been specified on the previous pages. A number of outlines are suggested by Daniel Goleman in his book, *Emotional Intelligence*. One of the most useful comes from Peter Salovey, a former Yale psychologist and current President of Yale University, whose list of emotional competencies includes a set of four abilities: Perceiving emotions, using emotions, understanding emotions, and managing emotions.

To be most effective, SEL content and processes should be applied consistently across the curriculum and at all grade levels. Students should be afforded many opportunities for skill practice, through a combination of dedicated activities and the countless unplanned "teachable moments" that occur daily. When emotional lessons are repeated over and over, they are reflected in strengthened neural pathways in the brain. They become positive habits that surface in times of stress.

Sharing Circles:
The SEL Super Strategy

Relationships are the heart of social emotional learning. The Sharing Circle process has been used for decades in classrooms and counseling groups to create a sense of community and to lay the foundation of a safe, caring learning environment while also specifically teaching such SEL skills as self-awareness, self-management, social-awareness, and relationship skills. In Sharing Circles the students and their teacher (or counselor) get to know each other on a meaningful, supportive level while discussing relevant topics dealing with the wide range of social emotional skill development.

A key avenue to maintaining and enhancing our social and emotional lives is through the process of verbal interaction. With our complex emotional and relational lives, it would be devastating if we couldn't talk with others about such things as our experiences, feelings, hopes, fears, desires etc. When we do share our experiences and feelings at a level beyond superficiality, we come to realize that all of us not only experience all of the emotions and feelings, but that we each experience them in our own unique ways. By sharing meaningful experiences and feelings in a safe space we are enabled to see the basic commonalities among us, and the individual differences too. This understanding leads to self-awareness and self-respect. On this foundation we can then develop empathy and concern for others as well. The benefits of time devoted to Sharing Circles are a growing awareness of self and an understanding of the importance of effectively relating to others.

How Sharing Circles Teach Social and Emotional Learning

As students follow the rules and relate to each other verbally during the Sharing Circle, they are practicing respectful listening and oral communication. As they listen carefully while other students and their teacher or counselor ponder and discuss the various topics, the students have repeated opportunities to mentally take the perspective of others. In doing so they grow to understand that others have joys and pains and fears just as they do. This lays the foundation for developing empathy and kindness. The ground rules also require them to demonstrate awareness and control over their own feelings, thoughts, and behaviors during the discussion. Through this repeated experience of positive give and take, they learn the importance of interacting responsibly and effectively while also practicing the valuable skill of self-management.

As students learn to relate effectively to others, issues related to acceptable and unacceptable behavior surface again and again. Students learn that all people have the power to influence one another. They become aware not only of how others affect them, but of the effects their behaviors have on others.

All students bring their own cultural and individual experiences to school. Sharing Circles provide an ideal way to give everyone repeated opportunities to express and share their individuality in a safe and accepting environment. When young people from differing cultural backgrounds, abilities and gender identities share truthful, respectful and meaningful discussions, it breaks down unconscious biases and fosters relationships and understanding. This is the true spirit of community building. In the Sharing Circle respect is always given and individual differences and cultural backgrounds are recognized and valued. Additionally, by getting to know their students in such a meaningful and personal way teachers and counselors can identify unique skills and experiences to build upon and areas of growth and needed support.

The Sharing Circle process has been designed so that healthy, responsible behaviors are modeled by the teacher or counselor in their role as the Sharing Circle leader. Also, the rules require that the students relate responsibly and effectively to one another. The process brings out and affirms the positive qualities inherent in everyone and allows students to practice effective modes of communication. Because Sharing Circles provide a place where participants are listened to and their feelings accepted, students learn how to provide the same conditions to peers and adults in interactions beyond the Sharing Circle sessions.

Sharing Circles teach cooperation and promote caring. As equitably as possible, the structure attempts to meet the needs of all participants. Everyone's feelings are accepted; everyone's contributions are judged valuable. The Sharing Circle is not another competitive arena, but is guided by a spirit of collaboration. When students practice fair, respectful interaction with one another, they benefit from the experience and are likely to employ these responsible behaviors in other life situations.

How To Conduct Sharing Circles

Sharing Circle Rules

1. Everyone gets a turn to share, including the leader.
2. You can skip your turn if you wish.
3. Listen to the person who is sharing.
4. There are no interruptions, put-downs, or gossip.
5. Share the time equally so everyone gets a turn to speak.

Steps for Leading a Sharing Circle

1. **State the Topic,** and then **set the stage by elaborating on the topic.** Make the topic relevant to your students. Tap into their life experiences and prior learning (Suggested elaborations are provided with each Sharing Circle Topic.).

2. **Facilitate the Sharing.** Make sure everyone who wants to share gets a turn to speak and is listened to respectfully and without interruption. Remind the students that there are no put-downs or gossip. What is said in the circle stays in the circle. Also, be sure to take your turn.

3. **Ask questions for reflection and learning.** At the conclusion of the Sharing phase, ask open-ended questions to stimulate thought and free discussion regarding the concepts, lessons, and other connections that can be made as a result of the sharing (Each Sharing Circle topic includes two or more discussion questions.).

Here is a more detailed look at the process of leading a Sharing Circle.

A Sharing Circle begins when a group of students and their leader (the teacher, or counselor) meet together in a group. The leader briefly greets and welcomes the students, conveying a feeling of enthusiasm blended with seriousness.

During the first few sessions and while the students are still learning about the rules, the leader takes a few moments to review the rules. These rules inform the students of the positive behaviors required of them and guarantees the emotional safety and security, and equality of each member.

When everyone has settled in and after the students understand and agree to follow the rules, the leader announces the topic for the session. A brief elaboration of the topic follows in which the leader provides examples and possibly mentions the topics relationship to prior topics or to other things the students are involved in. Then the leader re-states the topic and allows a little silence during which the students may review and ponder their own related memories and mentally prepare their verbal response to the topic. (The topics and brief elaborations are provided in this book.)

Next, the leader invites the students to voluntarily share their responses to the topic, one at a time. No one is forced to share (because it's okay to pass) but everyone is given an opportunity to share while all the other group members listen attentively. The participants tell the group about themselves, their personal experiences, thoughts, feelings, hopes and dreams as they relate to the topic. The most time in each session is devoted to this sharing phase because of its central importance.

During this time, the leader assumes a dual role—that of leader and participant. The leader makes sure that everyone who wishes to speak is given the opportunity while simultaneously enforcing the rules as necessary. The leader also takes a turn to speak if they wish.

After everyone who wants to share has done so, the leader introduces the next phase of the Sharing Circle by asking several discussion questions. This phase represents a transition to the intellectual mode and allows participants to reflect on and express learnings gained from the sharing phase and encourages participants to combine cognitive abilities and emotional experiencing. It's in this phase that participants are able to crystallize learnings and to understand the relevance of the discussion to their daily lives. (Discussion questions for each topic are provided in this book.)

When the students have finished discussing their responses to the questions and the session has reached a natural closure, the leader ends the session by thanking the students for being part of the Sharing Circle and stating that it is over.

Setting the Tone

The Sharing Circle provides a threat-free atmosphere where the students can explore their own feelings, thoughts and behaviors and consider those of the other members of the group. When you exhibit a positive, warm, and enthusiastic attitude, the students will know that this group is an important part of the day's learning experience, and most importantly that you care about them as individuals. By using the following communication techniques it will help to establish the rapport you are seeking and provide the foundation of a caring, supportive relationship.

- Use their names
- Show them that you are listening and hear what they are saying
- Let them know you think highly of them and their willingness to participate
- Make a conscientious effort to promote self-esteem and confidence. The Sharing Circle is a place where everyone has the "right" answer and should always feel successful in their participation whether by speaking or simply listening.

Review the Sharing Circle rules

At the beginning of the first few sessions, and if necessary at intervals thereafter, go over the ground rules. From this point on demonstrate to the students that you expect them to remember and abide by these rules. Convey to the students that you think well of them and know they are fully capable of responsible behavior. Let them know that by coming to the Circle they are making a commitment to listen and show acceptance and respect for the other students and you. It can be helpful to display the rules on the board or chart paper.

State and elaborate on the topic

State the topic and, then in your own words, elaborate and provide examples as each Sharing Circle lesson suggests. The topic can also be written on the board so that the students can review the topic as they need throughout the session. You may want to expand your elaboration beyond the brief suggestions provided with more examples. This elaboration of the topic is designed to get students focused and thinking about how they will respond to the topic. By providing more than just the mere statement of the topic, the elaboration gives students a few moments to expand their thinking and to make a personal connection to the topic at hand. Add clarifying statements of your own that will help the students understand the topic. Answer questions about the topic, and emphasize that there are no "right" or "wrong" responses. Finally, open the session to responses (theirs and yours). Sometimes taking your turn first helps the students understand the aim of the topic. The Sharing Circle elaborations, as written in this book, are provided to give you some general ideas for opening the Sharing Circle. It's important that you adjust, expand and modify the elaboration to suit the ages, abilities, levels, cultural/ethnic backgrounds and interests of your students.

Sharing by circle members

The most important point to remember is this: The purpose of these Sharing Circles is to give students an opportunity to express themselves and be accepted for the experiences, thoughts, and feelings they share. Keep the focus on the students. They are the stars!

Ask discussion questions

Responding to discussion questions is the cognitive portion of the process. During this phase, the leader asks thought-provoking questions to stimulate free discussion and higher-level thinking. As John Dewey, the early 20th century educational leader and reformer said "We do not learn from experience, we learn from reflecting on experience". Each Sharing Circle lesson concludes with several culminating discussion questions designed to foster reflection and self-awareness. You may want to formulate your own questions that are based on students' responses, relevant learning's you would like to focus on, or that are more appropriate to the level of understanding in your students. Use your professional judgment to determine exactly what questions to ask.

Close the circle

The ideal time to end a session is when the discussion question phase reaches natural closure. Sincerely thank everyone for being part of the group. Don't thank specific students for speaking, as doing so might convey the impression that speaking is more appreciated than listening. You could also thank the students for positive behaviors that were demonstrated during the session.

Self-Awareness

Significant People Who Have Affected My Life
Creative Writing and Discussion

Objectives: The students will:
—describe one or more people who have been influential in their lives.
—discuss the impact of significant people on their beliefs and behaviors.

Materials: writing materials for each student

Procedure: Begin by discussing with the class how people can strongly affect other people's lives. Individuals whom we admire and respect become models. Through their bad examples, other people teach us how *not* to be.

Explain the writing assignment. Point out that they will be writing about matters that are somewhat private. Ask them to think and write about one or more people who have significantly affected their lives, positively or negatively. Tell them to describe how each individual affected their beliefs, values, attitudes, habits, and/or goals. Add that in the cases of people who have had a negative influence, names and relationships should be omitted.

Have the students form pairs, triads, or small groups and share their thoughts about the people who have significantly affected their lives. (Remind them to omit the names and relationships of those people who have affected them negatively.)

After the students have shared in the small groups, facilitate a class discussion by asking the following and/or your own questions:

Discussion Questions:
1. What did you notice about how people can affect our lives positively? negatively?
2. How much of who you are seems to be influenced by other people?
3. If someone influences you, what part do you play in the changes that take place in you?
4. Can you think of anyone who would say that you have been a significant person in their life?

Learning About Ourselves
Experience Sheet and Discussion

Objectives: The students will:
— identify likes and dislikes and areas of strength and weakness.
— clarify personal values.
— explain how self-awareness facilitates performance.

Materials: one copy of the experience sheet "Who Am I," for each student

Procedure: Begin by discussing with the students the value of self-awareness and what it is. Explain that self-awareness is being aware of your feelings, thoughts and behaviors. It is knowing your strengths and challenges, values and goals. With self-awareness you are better able to improve aspects of your life. The more you know about yourself the better you are at getting along in life. Self-awareness helps you understand where you can make changes and build on your strengths and also helps you identify areas you can improve upon.

Next distribute the experience sheets and have the students answer the questions. When they have finished, break the students into small groups of three or four and have them each select a few of their responses to share with their group. Circulate and make sure everyone gets a chance to share. After this, facilitate a class discussion by asking these and your own questions to help the students reflect on their learning.

Discussion Questions:
1. What have you learned about your strengths and weaknesses from this activity?
2. What have you learned about your likes and dislikes?
3. What insights did you gain concerning your values?
4. How does knowing these kinds of things about yourself help you in school? ...in life?
5. How does knowing yourself help you get along with other people?
6. Do you think that by understanding yourself you can also understand others better? Explain your thinking.

Extend the learning: Use any of the writing prompts in the Experience Sheet as a Sharing Circle topic.

Who Am I?
Experience Sheet

An important element of successful living is knowing who you are. In order to have life goals that are meaningful, realistic, and achievable, you need an accurate sense of self-understanding. You need to know your strengths and limitations, likes and dislikes, wants and needs, beliefs and values. The following questions will help you clarify these things.

Think back to some of the things you've learned to do in life. The following questions will get you started:

• What are some things you've learned quickly and easily? (List at least three. These do not have to be school subjects.)

1. _____

2. _____

3. _____

• What is something that you learned because you kept working at it, even though it was hard? _____

• What are some things you do well that you could show other people how to do?
_____

• What are your major talents (strengths, abilities)?
_____

• In what school subject or activity are you most successful?
_____

What about weaknesses? First of all, everybody's got them. You aren't alone. Here are some things that other kids have trouble with. Put a ✔ beside any that you think apply to you. If you think of something that's not on this list, write it on the last line.

___ 1. Using my time well

___ 2. Standing up for myself when I know I am right

___ 3. Overcoming shyness

___ 4. Building self-confidence

___ 5. Giving myself credit for achievements

___ 6. Giving myself credit for strengths

___ 7. Learning from my mistakes

___ 8. Acknowledging my present weaknesses

___ 9. Starting a conversation with a member of the opposite sex

___10. _____

Admirable Qualities

List the ten qualities (such as honesty, bravery, helpfulness) you most admire in people.

1. _____   6. _____

2. _____   7. _____

3. _____   8. _____

4. _____   9. _____

5. _____ 10. _____

Something to think about: How many of the qualities you listed do your friends have? _____ How many do you have? _____

What does that mean to you? _____

_____

Now, complete the following half-sentences. Don't worry about being scrupulously honest or making perfect sense. Just have a good time looking at you.

One thing I wish others could know about me is _____

One of the things I feel proud of is _____

A thing I accept in myself is _____

A thing I can't accept in others is _____

One thing that makes me angry is _____

The way I usually handle my angry feelings is _____

The way I most need to improve is _____

I am happy when _____

I am sad when _____

I am fearful when _____

I feel lonely when _____

I get excited when _____

Something I don't know how to do (or don't understand) that I would like to learn _____

Something I like about myself that I woudn't change _____

Something You Wouldn't Know About Me...
Sharing and Discussion

Objectives: The students will:
—share something unusual about themselves.
—describe what it feels like to share something about themselves that is neither obvious or generally known.

Materials: white board

Procedure: Write this topic on the board:

> Something You Wouldn't Know About Me Unless I Told You

In your own words, say to the students: *We already know many things about each other and with time we will get to know each other better and better — with each other's ideas, feelings, experiences, hopes, and concerns. However, just for the fun of it today, let's tell each other something that wouldn't normally come up in our everyday interactions. When it's your turn think of something unusual, funny, offbeat, or peculiar about yourself to tell us. For instance, maybe you like to invent things, collect old mystery books, sleep with your pet iguana, or read the dictionary for fun. Perhaps you have a famous relative, know a foolproof cure for hiccups, or sing with gusto when you're alone. You can tell us just about anything as long as it's something we probably wouldn't learn otherwise.*

Begin the process by telling something about yourself. Model the desired spirit by sharing something light and humorous. Then, go around the group and give each student an opportunity to speak.

If time permits, invite volunteers to prove their listening skills by repeating the names of people in the group and restating the information those people shared. If you do this part of the activity be sure everyone has their contribution repeated back to them.

Culminate the sharing by asking these and your own questions.

Discussion Questions:
1. How did it feel to talk about something that was not generally known about you?
2. Why do you suppose we don't generally learn these things about each other?
3. Did you notice any similarities or differences between what was shared?

How We See Ourselves
Self-Assessment, Sharing, and Discussion

Objectives: The students will:
—rate the degree to which they possess specific qualities or characteristics.
—represent their self-concept pictorially or in words.
—describe how self-concept affects daily living.

Materials: one copy of the experience sheet, "Looking at Me" for each student; colored markers for students who choose to draw an image of themselve

Procedure: Begin with a brief discussion about self-concept. Explain that self-concept is the image we have of ourselves. It's like looking in the mirror, except that the image we have depends more on our thoughts and conclusions about ourselves than it does on the physical self we see in the mirror. Point out that people often see themselves quite differently than others see them.

Distribute the experience sheets and briefly review the directions. Give the students time to complete the sheet. Make colored marking pens available to students who wish to draw pictures of themselves instead of writing paragraphs.

If the group is large, have the students form smaller groupings (three to five) and share their self-assessments and drawings/paragraphs. If the group is small, complete this part of the activity as a total group. Emphasize that all sharing is voluntary, and that students may keep any or all parts of the experience sheet confidential if they choose. Conclude the activity by facilitating further discussion about self-concept with the entire group.

Discussion Questions:
1. Did you learn anything about yourself from this activity that surprised you? What was it?
2. What strengths did your self-assessment reveal?
3. What qualities would you like to develop more of?
4. What qualities would you like to reduce or eliminate?
5. What qualities or concerns did you discover you have in common with other members of the group?
6. How does self-concept affect our performance at school? ...our relations with other people? ...our outlook on life in general and the future?

Self-Awareness

Looking at Me
Self-Assessment

Read through the list of characteristics below. Decide how well each characteristic fits YOU. Be honest. If you are unsure about an item, ask yourself how others see you. Circle the point on the scale that describes you best.

	Most of the time		Average		Almost never

1. Well-liked
2. Good looking
3. Intelligent
4. Popular
5. Athletic
6. Appreciated
7. Talented
8. Happy
9. Worried
10. Relaxed
11. Caring
12. Strong
13. Unique
14. Assertive
15. Enthusiastic
16. Energetic
17. Tense
18. Dependable
19. A good friend
20. Boring
21. Tough
22. Confident
23. Unhappy
24. Creative
25. A leader
26. Friendly
27. Helpful
28. Responsible
29. Fun
30. Angry
31. Honest
32. Successful
33. A loner
34. Shy
35. Generous

On the other side of this paper, draw a picture or write a paragraph that describes your thoughts and feelings about yourself.

Four Concepts
Creative Self-Assessment and Discussion

Objectives: The students will:
—distinguish between how others see them and how they see themselves.
—distinguish between present self-concept and desired self-concept.

Materials: one copy of the experience sheet, "Concepts of Me" for each student; marking pens in various colors

Procedure: Remind the students of the definition of self-concept that was discussed in the previous activity. (You may wish to distinguish between self-concept and self-esteem. Self-concept is one's **view** of self; self-esteem is the **value** placed on that view.)

Distribute the experience sheets, and place the marking pens where the students can share them. Go over the directions printed on the sheet. Emphasize that the students may employ descriptive word lists, paragraph descriptions, illustrations, symbols — even poetry — to complete their four descriptions. Suggest they begin with quadrant 1, and do the rest in any sequence they wish.

Allow sufficient time for thinking and creativity. When the students have finished, have them read (or show) and explain their descriptions to the group. After the students have shared, ask these and your own questions to facilitate discussion and reflection.

Discussion Questions:
1. Why do others see us differently than we see ourselves?
2. If you asked your best friend to describe you, which quadrant would their description match most closely? Why?
3. Which quadrants do you wish were more similar?
4. What can you do to bring those images closer together?

Self-Awareness

Concepts of Me
Experience Sheet

Your *self-concept* is how you *view* yourself. It is what you *think about* yourself. Other people also have a concept of you. In the spaces below, write or draw four descriptions (concepts) of you. Notice their similarities and differences.

1. The concept *I* have of myself:	3. The concept *I would like* to have of myself:
2. The concept *others* have of me:	4. The concept *I would like others* to have of me:

Creating a Metaphor Name
Individual Creativity and Group Discussion

Objectives: The students will:
— identify an aspect of their self-concept that they wish to project.
— create a name to represent that aspect.
— describe the power and significance of names.

Materials: Art paper; colored marking pens

Procedure: Begin the activity by discussing with the students the importance of names. Make these points:
- Most of us have no choice about our name — it is selected before or at the time of our birth.
- Our name is as much a part of us as our eyes, teeth, or hands. We can't see or touch it, but it is always there.
- Our name represents *everything* that is known about us. Just like the name *Disney* creates a mental image of hundreds of movies, videos, cartoon characters and recreational acres, our name creates an image that encompasses our totality.
- Some of us don't like our names.

Go around the group and ask the students to share something about their name: who they were named after; their middle name; a problem their name causes; why their parents picked that name; etc.

Next, ask the students: *How many of us are happy with our names?*

Tell the students that since names are so important, they are going to have an opportunity to create their own name — a *metaphor* name. Explain that a metaphor name stands for something about the person who bears it. It creates a mental picture that is in keeping with some aspect of that person's self-concept. Give several examples: Quiet River, Soaring Eagle, Light Sleeper; Digital Dancer; Chameleon Child.

Urge the students to create a name that truly represents them. Give them plenty of time to do this. Encourage students who like to bounce their ideas off of others to interact quietly. Distribute the art paper and markers. Have the students write or print their metaphor name on the paper, adding a symbol or picture of themselves that illustrates the significance of their name if they wish.

Go around the group and taking turns have each student hold up the paper with their metaphor name and symbol on it and explain the significance of the metaphor name they created. When the students have finished sharing lead a group discussion by asking these and your own questions.

Discussion Questions:

1. How can a name help or hurt our self-concept?
2. Would you ever consider changing your name? Why or why not?
3. What other things about yourself would you like to change? Would they be harder or easier to change than your name?
4. If you want to project the image of your metaphor name, in what other ways can you do it?
5. What have you learned about self-concept from this activity?

WHO I AM CULTURALLY
Discussion and Experience Sheet

Objectives: The students will:
—discuss the components of culture
—share personally meaningful aspects of their cultural heritage
—discuss the importance of cultural influences and of respecting other cultures

Materials: One copy of the experience sheet, "Who I am Culturally" for each student

Procedure: Begin the activity by discussing what culture is and how it influences us. The discussion should help the students develop a basic concept of what makes up culture. If using America as an example talk about such things as the primary language, what foods people eat, how people dress, values held in common (democracy, liberty, etc,) and what symbols represent America. Help the students to understand that culture means all the ways people live together and define themselves.

Next, pass out the experiences sheets. Review the directions and provide time for the students to complete their sheets. Circulate and provide any help needed.

When the students have completed their experience sheets break them into small groups and ask them to share some of the important cultural influences they have written about.

After all the students have had an opportunity to share in their small groups bring the entire class together. Culminate the activity by asking these and/or your own discussion questions to help the students reflect on their learning.

Discussion Questions:

1. Why is it a good thing for us to be proud of our cultural heritage?
2. How does it help us to understand each other better when we know something about all our cultural backgrounds?
3. Did you learn anything new about someone from this activity?
4. Did you learn anything about another culture that you didn't know before?
5. Do you have to be born into another culture to understand it… to appreciate it? Explain.
6. What are some of the many ways we benefit by living in a culturally diverse society?

WHO I AM CULTURALLY
Experience Sheet

Think about the many ways your culture has influenced you and helped to make you the person you are. There are many elements that make up a culture. Below are just a few significant cultural areas for you to consider how they have influenced your life.

My cultural heritage is _____

The predominate language of my culture is _____

FOOD

What are some of your favorite foods, or special dishes, that you enjoy?

_____ _____

_____ _____

_____ _____

MUSIC

How does the music of your culture make you feel? _____

_____

Do you have a favorite song? _____

_____

CUSTOMS AND TRADITIONS

In your culture how do you acknowledge ...

Birthdays. _____

_____

Weddings. _____

_____

Birth of a child. _____

_____

A death. _____

_____

Describe other customs or traditions of your culture. _____

_____

HOLIDAYS

What holidays do you celebrate? _____
_____

What is your favorite holiday? _____

How do you celebarate your favorite holiday? _____
_____
_____

RELIGION

Do you have a religious ritual you find meaningful? _____
Describe it and how it makes you feel.
_____
_____
_____
_____
_____

VALUES

Identify some of the important values of your cultural heritage. _____
_____
_____
_____
_____
_____
_____

SPECIAL TO YOU

List some of the things you're happy to have in your life because of your culture.
_____
_____
_____
_____
_____

A Significant Event in My Life
A Sharing Circle

Objectives: The students will:
—identify important moments in their lives.
—describe the role their feelings play in determining the importance of an event.

Introduce the Topic: In your own words say to the students: *Our topic is, "A Significant Event in My Life." There are many kinds of events that hold places of significance in our memories. What is one of the most significant that you can recall? It could be an achievement, such as winning an academic or athletic event or mastering a skill, or it could be a personal triumph, such as gaining control of a habit. Your significant event might be a move you made to new city or school. Or it might be a negative event, such as the death of a pet, or a divorce in the family. Think of one event in your life that you would like to share. Our topic is, "A Significant Event in My Life."*

Discussion Questions:

1. How do you know whether an event in your life is significant or insignificant?
2. Who decides how much importance an event has?
3. How do you think you will feel in five or ten years about events that are significant to you now?

Self-Awareness

How I Got Someone to Pay Attention to Me
A Sharing Circle

Objectives: The students will:
—verbalize the importance of receiving interpersonal attention.
—state the importance of paying attention as a skill.
—identify positive, effective strategies for getting attention.

Introduce the Topic: In your own words say to the students: *Our topic for this session is "How I Got Someone to Pay Attention to Me." When you or I want to communicate with someone, first of all we have to get the person to notice us. We have to do something to get the other person to focus on us. As you have probably noticed, there are many ways to do this. You can do something funny, helpful, destructive, informative, exciting, or whatever, and people will automatically look at you.*

You are invited to share a time when you got someone's attention in a particular situation. Perhaps you tried to get the attention of a person who was a long way away from you in a large crowd. Or perhaps the person whose attention you were trying to get was watching TV or doing something else nearby. Think about it for a few moments. The topic is, "How I Got Someone to Pay Attention to Me."

Discussion Questions:
1. Do people really need attention?
2. Does the way you get attention have anything at all to do with the kind of attention you get or how long the attention lasts?
3. What do you think a person would be like who never got any attention?
4. What does giving your attention have to do with good communication?
5. What did the other person seem to think of your attention-getting method?

An Ability or Talent I'm Proud of
A Sharing Circle

Objectives: The students will:
—describe an ability or talent.
—discuss the importance of acknowledging one's own strengths and abilities.
—demonstrate appreciation for the abilities of others.

Introduce the Topic: In your own words say to the students: *This is going to be an unusual circle session because we are going to encourage each other to do something most people don't do very often. We're going to take credit for things we're good at. Most of the time people are modest, but today we will ignore any rules of modesty we've learned, which will probably do us good. The topic is, "An Ability or Talent I'm Proud of."*

It's obvious that everyone has strengths and weaknesses. No one is good at everything and no one is poor at everything. Think for a minute about those things at which you are just naturally good. Think about your special skills. Maybe you excel in an academic area like Math, Science, or English. Or perhaps you have an athletic skill you're proud of. Maybe you have artistic talents, or are good at making things with your hands. You might have inherited your abilities from your parents, or you may be the only one in your family who has them. Think it over for a few moments. The topic is, "An Ability or Talent I'm Proud of."

Discussion Questions:
1. How did we feel telling each other about our abilities and talents? Did it feel a bit like bragging?
2. What benefits do we get from talking about our strengths and abilities?
3. How did you feel about each other during this session?
4. How did you develop your strengths and abilities?

A Special Occasion or Holiday That Relates to My Culture
A Sharing Circle

Objectives: The students will:
—describe a traditional event that they observe and explain its significance.
—discuss the role of tradition in life and explain how they benefit from honoring their cultural traditions.

Introduce the Topic: In your own words say to the students: *In today's circle, we're going to talk about something that belongs to your culture or cultural heritage. The topic is, "A Special Occasion or Holiday That Relates to My Culture." Some special occasions are referred to in English as "rites of passage." Events like the christening of a baby, a baptism, bat/bar mitzvah, wedding, or funeral mark a person's passage from one stage in life to another. Not every event of this nature is enjoyable, of course, but even funerals offer a kind of comfort to family members.*

Many of the values and attitudes handed down from one generation to another last a long time because they are a traditional part of a certain way of life; they stand for something treasured. Examples are the Fourth of July, Cinco de Mayo, Halloween, Easter, or Passover. Take a moment to think of a special occasion that relates to your culture — a rite of passage or a holiday — that you particularly enjoy and appreciate. The topic is, "A Special Occasion or Holiday That Relates to My Culture."

Discussion Questions:
1. What do holidays and rites of passage do for people?
2. Why is it important to honor cultural traditions?
3. How do you feel about doing traditional things that your ancestors did?
4. How does participating in these special occasions or holidays bring meaning to your life? ...give you a sense of identity?

One of My Favorite Possessions
A Sharing Circle

Objectives: The students will:
—become better acquainted with one another.
—identify feelings associated with favorite items.
—examine the values they hold that make something special to them.

Introduce the Topic: In your own words say to the students: *Our topic for today is, "One of My Favorite Possessions." You probably own several things that are special to you. You may have had some of these possessions since you were very young, and you may have acquired others more recently. Tell us about one thing you own that you really treasure, and tell us why this item means so much to you. Someone you care for very much may have given it to you, or you may have done extra chores to earn the money to buy it. Your favorite item could be a photograph, book, piece of jewelry, game, or a card that you received from someone. It could be something you wear, play with, work with, or decorate your room with. Think about it for a moment. The topic is, "One of My Favorite Possessions."*

Discussion Questions:
1. What is it that makes certain things important to us?
2. What feelings do you get when you think of a favorite possession?
3. Do you think it's important for people to have special possessions? Why or why not?
4. How do your values help you decide which of your possessions are favorites?

Self-Awareness 37

Something I Like to Imagine
A Sharing Circle

Objectives: The students will:
—identify the benefits of imagination
—recognize the creative power of imagination

Introduce the Topic: In your own words say to the students: *Our topic for this session is "Something I Like to Imagine." Did you know that using your imagination is a very healthy and important thing to do? You may find yourself daydreaming and not realize that what you're doing is necessary. You need to daydream and imagine things, even if what you are imaging seems absurd or ridiculous. So think about something you like to imagine. Maybe it's reliving an event from the past or imaging what it would be like to experience something you've never done. Perhaps it's a wish or a creative idea concerning something you'd like to make or write about. Or it could be a wild fantasy of some kind. Whatever it is, we would like to hear about it. The topic is, "Something I Like to Imagine."*

After the students have finished sharing, ask several open-ended questions to spark a discussion.

Discussion Questions:
1. In what ways do you think daydreaming and using your imagination help you to be creative?
2. What do you think people would be like if they had no powers of imagination?
3. Did you recognize anything about yourself by sharing what you like to imagine?
4. Did you learn something about someone in this session that you didn't know before?
5. What feelings do you experience when you imagine the thing you shared?
6. If you would like to create, or do the thing you like to imagine what are some things you can do to make it happen?

38   Self-Awareness

Self-Management

Change Your Thoughts — Change Your Feelings
Experience Sheet and Discussion

Objectives: The students will:
—describe the causal relationship between thoughts and feelings.
—state that their feelings in a situation can be improved by changing their thoughts about the situation.

Materials: one copy of the experience sheet, "Think Differently to Feel Differently" for each student; whiteboard

Procedure: On the board make three columns. Over the first column, write the heading, "Situation." Over the second, write the heading, "Thoughts" and over the third, write the heading, "Feelings."

Begin by asking the students to help you generate a list of situations that typically lead to negative feelings. Responses might include:
- not knowing the answer when the teacher calls on me
- doing poorly on a test for which I studied hard
- eating lunch alone
- not being invited to a friend's party
- being eliminated during tryouts for a team, musical group, cheer leading squad, school play, etc.
- when a boy/girl I like doesn't like me

List the situations in the first column. Then take one situation at a time and ask the students what thoughts a person might be likely to have in that situation. For example, a student who has to eat lunch alone might think, "I'm not fun (popular, attractive) enough." A student who doesn't know the answer to a teacher's question might think, "I always end up looking stupid." Write all suggestions in the second column.

Then ask the students how they would feel in each situation if they had the thoughts described. For example, a person eating alone who thinks she isn't popular might feel humiliated or depressed. The person who thinks he looks stupid because he can't answer a question might feel embarrassed or frustrated. Continue making connections between the thoughts and subsequent feelings in each situation.

Suggest to the students that the feelings in each situation can be improved by changing the thoughts from negative to neutral or positive. For example, what would happen to the feelings of the student who couldn't answer his teacher's question if he thought, "I don't know the answer, but I'll listen and find out what the answer is so I'll know it next time." <u>Make the point that situations don't cause feelings, thoughts cause feelings.</u> No one forces a person to feel a certain way in a particular situation. Suggest this idea: The easiest way to change your feelings about a situation is to change your thoughts about it.

Distribute the experience sheets. Give the students time to write down their ideas for positive thinking under each example. Then have them form small groups, discuss their responses, and collectively generate additional ideas about what thoughts could lead to more positive feelings in each situation. Have each small group share some of the thoughts they listed with the entire class. Culminate this by leading a follow-up discussion to help the students reflect on their learning.

Discussion Questions:

1. How do thoughts trigger feelings?
2. Why is it easier to change your thoughts about a situation than it is to change your feelings?
3. Why do we waste our time feeling miserable about things that we cannot change?
4. Who is in control of your thoughts? ... of your feelings?
5. What are some thoughts that can help you feel calm, upbeat and in control when something upsetting happens.

Self-Management 41

Think Differently to Feel Differently
Experience Sheet

What really causes people to feel the way they do? Is it the situation they are in or is it how they are thinking about the situation? Below are some common situations that kids your age often find themselves in. It's probably pretty easy to come up with some negative thoughts that would just make you feel worse. How could you choose to think in each situation that would help you feel more positive and optimistic? Write down your ideas under each situation.

1. You're running late for school and you miss your bus.

_____

_____

2. You don't get asked to the school dance.

_____

_____

3. You got sick and couldn't go to your friend's party.

_____

_____

4. Your poor score in the swim meet prevented your team from winning first place.

_____

_____

5. You didn't get chosen for the tennis team.

_____
_____

6. You studied hard for the big test but you only made a "C".

_____
_____

7. You have an argument with your best friend.

_____
_____

8. You'll be moving with your family to a new state.

_____
_____

9. Your new haircut didn't turn out like you wanted it to.

_____
_____

10. Your parents say you may not go to the concert with your friends.

_____
_____

What Comes Before Anger
Looking at Anger as a Secondary Emotion

Objectives: The students will:
—identify feelings that typically precede/precipitate anger and identify ways to deal with those feelings.
—practice acceptable ways to express "first feelings."

Materials: whiteboard

Procedure: Introduce this activity by explaining that anger is a normal emotion, experienced by everyone. However, anger tends to be a secondary emotion. In other words, one or more other feelings usually come before anger. These can be referred to as "first feelings." Give the students an example, such as: You forget to study for a test and fail it. Because the test covered a subject in which you usually do well, you feel disappointed and frustrated. However, those "first feelings" quickly turn to anger. Before you know it, anger is the only feeling that you are aware of and the only one other people observe in you.

Continue by introducing this second and related concept: Other people usually find it hard to deal with our anger. If we become hostile and aggressive when we are angry, we cause others to feel threatened and maybe even to get angry in return. Other people have an easier time responding to our first feeling of disappointment, frustration, embarrassment, grief, or fear. Consequently, a valuable skill to develop is the skill of identifying and expressing our initial feelings, rather than just our anger. To do this, we need to "buy time" in upsetting situations.

Ask the group to think of some initial emotions that often precede anger and write them on the board. They can include feelings such as sadness, grief, frustration, embarrassment, relief, shock, disappointment, and confusion. Then ask the students to suggest acceptable ways of expressing these feelings that others can identify with.

If you need to provide another example of this concept in action, read the following scenario to the group and ask them the questions that follow:

Maria was one of the best players on the hockey team. She really wanted to be captain the coming semester and had more than just a good chance of being elected. Her teammates liked and respected her and she got along well with her coach. Maria knew that her grades had to stay above a C and she struggled to keep her Social Studies grade up. Poor reading skills kept her from doing very well. When she took her final Social Studies test before semester's end, she thought she had done okay. When report cards came out, however, she saw a "D" in Social Studies. During hockey practice after school, Maria announced that she didn't want to be captain of the team. When her friends asked her why she had changed her mind, Maria snapped at them and said, "Who wants to be captain of this stupid team, anyway? I have better things to worry about than keeping you all in line."

—What were Maria's initial feelings?
—How did she express those feelings?
—How could Maria have better expressed her emotions?

Finally, invite the students to describe difficult and challenging situations that they've experienced recently — preferably ones in which they became angry. Ask them to think back to their very first emotional reaction to the incident and try to pinpoint what it was. This may be difficult for some students, particularly those who have a habit of erupting in anger at the first glimmer of upset or conflict. Keep digging, however. In most cases, other feelings are buried there.

Try role-playing the incident. Have the student play him or herself and another member of the group take the role of the other person involved. Employ the alter ego technique, by stationing an additional student next to the central character. Each time this person speaks, allow the alter ego to add comments that express possible thoughts and feelings.

Discussion Questions:

1. How does anger mask what is really going on inside someone?
2. Why is anger so difficult to deal with in other people?
3. Do you think people are sometimes afraid to show their first feelings? Why?
4. What have you learned about your own behaviors from this session?
5. How can this understanding of "first feelings" help you handle your angry feelings going forward?

Self-Management 45

Taking Charge of Personal Anger
Small Group Activity and Experience Sheet

Objectives: The students will:
—show how an upsetting event produces thoughts related to the event, which in turn produce feelings (often anger).
— state that a key to managing anger is buying time to think.
—practice substituting moderate thoughts for angry thoughts as one way of reducing anger.

Materials: whiteboard; a copy of the experience sheet "Thinking Differently" for each student

Procedure: Explain that the group is going to demonstrate how buying time will allow them the opportunity to change their thoughts about upsetting situations which in turn can reduce anger and bad feelings.

Write four headings across the top of the board: **Event**, **Thoughts**, **Feelings**, and **Substitute Thoughts**. Under the Event column write Mom won't let me go to the dance with my friends. Skip the second column and ask the students what their feelings might be in this situation. The students will probably suggest words such as mad, furious, and miserable. Write several of these words in the Feelings column. Then go back to the Thoughts column, and ask the students what their thoughts might be concerning the same situation. Elicit answers such as these: She's being mean or unreasonable. She doesn't understand how important it is to me. She never wants me to have fun.

Explain to the students that it is not the event, but the thoughts about the event that cause the feelings. Refer to the sentences in the second column and point out that any of these thoughts about the event could create angry feelings. Explain that no situation, event, or person makes us have a particular feeling. Through our thoughts, we choose our feelings, even if we are not aware of it.

Next, suggest that if the thoughts recorded in the second column can be moderated, the feelings too will change. Help the students create new thought statements such as: Mom thinks she is looking out for my safety. She has family plans the night of the

46   Self-Management

dance and wants me to be with the family. There will be more dances this year. Record them in the last column, Substitute Thoughts. Point out that these moderated thoughts will reduce the anger and bad feelings.

Pass out the Experience Sheets. Under the first heading, event, ask the students to list three real or hypothetical situations/events in which they are certain they would feel angry. In the second column (adjacent to each description), have them write the thoughts they would have in each situation. Then in the third column ask them to write down the feelings that these thoughts would create. Finally, challenge the students to come up with different thoughts that could be substituted for the original thoughts and write those in the fourth column.

When all of the students have completed their Experience Sheets, invite individuals to share their analysis of one conflict. After each example, ask the group how their feelings might change as a result of the substitute thoughts. Emphasize that when they find themselves reacting to a situation too strongly, they can improve the situation and their disposition by rethinking the situation. To do this, they need to buy time. Both abilities take practice and perseverance, but they work!

Complete this activity by teaching the students to remember the acronym **STOP** whenever they feel their anger or stress levels rising.

S = Stop what you are doing.
T = Take several deeep breaths.
O = Observe without judging what you're feeling and thinking.
P = Proceed with your day in a calm and in control manner.

Point out that this simple exercise will help them calm down in the moment, but it also helps to retrain their automatic response to anger and stress so they stay calmer in future situations.

Discussion Questions:
1. Why do we choose to feel angry in certain situations?
2. When you are angry, why is it important to "buy yourself some time" to rethink the situation?
3. What's the hardest thing about changing your thoughts in a situation?
4. What have you learned about your own anger from this session?

THINKING DIFFERENTLY
EXPERIENCE SHEET

EVENT	THOUGHTS	FEELINGS	SUBSTITUTE THOUGHTS

Mood Management Strategies
Experience Sheet and Discussion

Objectives: The students will:
—explain how moods are affected by feelings left over from conflicts and upsetting events.
—identify problems and feelings associated with specific events.
—describe strategies for releasing residual feelings and managing negative moods.

Materials: one copy of the experience sheet, "Three Lousy Moods," for each student; whiteboard; 3" x 5" index cards

Procedure: Begin by asking the students: *Have you ever been in an extremely bad mood because of something negative that happened in one relatively small area of your life?*

Invite volunteers to briefly share their "bad mood" experiences. Then, ask for a show of hands from students who have behaved badly toward a friend or family member for no particular reason other than they were in a bad mood. Point out that this sort of thing happens all the time.

Distribute the experience sheets and quickly go over the directions. Allow the students to work with partners to complete their sheets. Allow about 10 minutes.

When the students have completed their experience sheets, take a few minutes to discuss the three scenarios described. Looking at one scenario at a time, ask the students how they answered the questions. Help the students recognize and describe how Rita, Ahmad, and Mike each started with a specific problem or conflict which produced certain feelings (frustration, worry, disappointment, anxiety, embarrassment, etc.). In all three cases, these first feelings were followed by anger, and the anger carried over into unrelated activities involving unsuspecting friends.

Self-Awareness 49

Next, write the following guidelines on the board:

GUIDE TO MANAGING MOODS

1. BUY YOURSELF SOME TIME!!!!!
2. Fill this time with mood management strategies.
3. It takes time for feelings to go away naturally. Don't let them affect other activities.

Ask the students why it is so important to "buy time" when you are experiencing negative feelings associated with a problem or conflict?

Facilitate a discussion around the three guidelines, inviting input and examples from the students, and making these points:

- The feelings we take away from a problem or conflict (residual feelings) tend to stay with us for some time. Even a well-managed conflict is stressful, and left over feelings can carry over into other activities and relationships. In addition, they can be hard on us physically.
- Internal conflicts, or conflicts that cannot be immediately resolved for one reason or another, also produce stress. Negative feelings may be with us constantly until the problem is resolved.
- Residual feelings and feelings associated with unresolved conflict affect our moods.
- The use of mood-management strategies can help us relieve stress and negative feelings, lessening the chance that a "bad mood" will result in damage to our body, our relationships, and other areas of our life.

On the board, write the heading, "Mood Management Strategies." Ask the students to help you brainstorm positive, healthy ways of releasing anger and other negative feelings.

Include items such as:

- Talk with a trusted friend or adult.
- Run laps around the block or track.
- Leave the situation and take several slow, deep breaths.
- Get something to eat or drink.
- Listen to relaxing music.
- Take a walk in a pleasant natural setting.
- Imagine being in a favorite place.
- Work on a project or hobby.

NOTE: Venting anger and the idea of "blowing off steam" have been found to not diminish negative emotions but they often make things worse. Activities that calm the body and mind get us out of a state of threat and are the strategies being looked for.

Divide the students into groups of 3 or 4. Give each student a 3" x 5" card. Have the students discuss the pro's and con's of different mood management strategies listed on the board. Tell them to also discuss any ideas that are in addition to what you listed on the board. Tell the students to each pick three or four mood management ideas that they think might work for them and to write their choices on their cards. Encourage them to carry the card with them, or tape it to a mirror or closet door at home as a reminder of what strategies they can use when faced with conflicts or upsetting situations.

Culminate the activity by asking these and your own questions to help the students reflect on their learning..

Discussion Questions:
1. Why is it important to be aware of the feelings we have that come before anger?
2. What are some of the most common mood management startegies that were identified
3. Why is it important to identify some mood management startegies that you think will work for you?
4. How easy, or hard, do you think is will be to engage yourself in a mood management strategy when you're feeling upset? Explain.

Extend the Learning: In subsequent sessions, ask volunteers to report on their progress using mood management strategies. Frequently remind the students that these strategies are short-term controls, not permanent solutions to big problems. However, they do relieve stress, calm us down, and allow us to enter into problem solving and conflict resolution with greater self-control and productivity.

Three Lousy Moods
Student Experience Sheet

Read the following scenarios. Write your answers to the questions on the lines provided.

Scenario 1:

Rita was ready to leave for school, but she couldn't find her books and nobody seemed to know where they were. She had two assignments due that day and both were inside her books. She started to get upset. After nearly thirty minutes of searching, Rita found the books in one of her little sister, Martha's, favorite hiding places. When she confronted her, Martha admitted hiding them. Even though she found her books, Rita was still mad at her sister and left for school late and in a terrible mood. When she walked into her first class, her best friend Cathy said, "Hi girl, you look upset." Rita snapped, "Leave me alone, I don't want to talk to you!"

—What was Rita's real problem?
_____

—What were her first feelings about that problem?
_____

—What were some of her other feelings?
_____

—What did Cathy do that caused Rita to respond the way she did?
_____

—Why did Rita snap at Cathy?
_____

Scenario 2:

Ahmad was just finishing a report on the computer when he hit the wrong key and erased all of his work. He felt totally frustrated and starting to get angry with himself, but he had to get to his next class. Ahmad walked out of the computer room and down the hall. Lost in his thoughts about doing something so stupid, he stumbled right into Judy, knocking her books all over the floor. Then he gave her a disgusted look and yelled, "Why don't you look where you're going."

—What was Ahmad's real problem?

—What were his first feelings about that problem?

—What were some of his other feelings?

—What did Judy do that caused Ahmad to behave toward her the way he did?

—Why did Ahmad yell at Judy?

Scenario 3:

Mike just found out that he didn't make the final cut for the basketball team. As he walked away from the gym, he started feeling angry. Mike thought it was unfair that some of the guys who did make the team couldn't shoot or maneuver nearly as well as he could. He felt crummy. When he walked around the corner, Mike saw a bunch of his friends talking. When Charlie saw Mike, he said, "What are you looking so down about?" Mike was embarrassed. He didn't want anyone to know he'd been cut, so all he said was, "None of your business," and walked off.

—What was Mike's real problem?

—What were his first feelings about that problem?

—What were some of his other feelings?

—What did Charlie do that caused Mike to behave the way he did?

—Why was Mike rude to his friends, and why did he just walk off?

Causes of Anger
Experience Sheet and Discussion

Objectives:	Students will: --Identify people, conditions, and situations that tend to make them angry. --Describe constructive ways to manage their anger.
Materials:	One copy of the experience sheet "What Sets Me Off" for each student
Procedure:	Engage the students in a discussion about anger. Acknowledge that it is an uncomfortable emotion that can sometimes be difficult to control. However, emphasize that it is normal to feel angry at times, and that anger can play a useful role in day-to-day life. Make these additional points: • Anger is a normal human emotion. • Anger itself is neither bad nor good. It's how we manage our anger that can make a difference. • Sometimes anger serves a protective function. • Volatile expressions of anger, especially if they happen often, can have negative consequences. • There are healthy and appropriate ways to manage anger. • It is how we react to a situation, not the situation itself, that causes anger and other emotions. Distribute the experience sheets and go over the directions. Give the students a few minutes to list situations and conditions that make them angry and ways to manage the anger. When they have finished, ask volunteers to read some of their items to the group. Elaborate on each example and use it to generate further discussion. Focus less on the situations (and their justification) and more on anger-management strategies.
Discussion Questions:	1. Why is it important to control anger? 2. What are the most common causes of anger in our group? 3. What ideas for controlling anger work best for you? 4. What new ideas for controlling anger would you like to try? 5. What can you do if nothing you try helps to lessen your anger?

What Sets Me Off
Experience Sheet

Do certain things almost always make you angry? Do you react angrily to the same situations—or the same people—over and over? Maybe you get angry when you don't get your way. Or when your brother or sister uses your things without asking. In the left column, list things that usually make you angry. In the right column, list things you can do to deal with your angry feelings in constructive ways.

What Makes Me Angry	**What I Can Do To Be In Control of Myself and My Feelings**
1.	
2.	
3.	
4.	
5.	
6.	
7.	
8.	
9.	
10.	

Setting and Attaining Goals
Discussion and Experience Sheet

Objectives: The students will:
—explain that having a goal is the first step to achieving what one wants.
—identify specific steps for attaining goals.
—develop skills in setting practical and achievable goals.
—experience goal attainment.

Materials: pens or pencils, blank note paper, the experience sheets, "You Can Reach Your Goals!" and "Tips for Setting Goals" (one copy for each student)

Procedure: This is a continuing activity designed to be used with students over several weeks. In addition to learning an effective goal-setting process it will allow them to experience the satisfaction of setting and achieving goals and recognizing the self-management skills necessary to stay on track to achievement.

Introduce the activity. Explain to the students that most successful people have a habit of setting clear goals concerning things that they want to accomplish. Explain that in this activity, the students will set goals and experience the feeling of success that comes with attaining them.

Point out that when we think of goals, we usually picture big, important things like cars, houses, vacations, etc., but that we set dozens of smaller goals each day. Provide several examples of things you want to achieve today then ask volunteers to share some of the things they want to accomplish today. Point out that stating these things is the simplest form of goal setting.

Distribute the experience sheets. Begin by discussing the "Tips for Setting Goals" making sure the students understand each of the 7 tips. Next review PART 1 of the goal-setting experience sheet. Then give the students time to complete the first part of the sheet, writing down three goals and identifying if they are short term or long term and the target date for achievement. Remind the students to refer to the "Tips for Setting Goals" as they write their goals down.

If possible, spend a few moments with each student, reviewing his or her goals to make sure that they are attainable, properly written, and within the purview of the student to achieve (not dependent on events or people outside the student's control).

When the students have completed PART 1 move on to PART 2 the "Goal Achievement Score Sheet". Explain that goals are achieved in steps. Success is measured as each step is completed. Point out that PART 2 of the experience sheet helps the students break down their goals into more easily managed steps. Point out that they should regularly review their progress on each step and to check whether the step was achieved or not at each review

Allow time for the students to identify and write down the steps for each of their goals. While they are writing, offer assistance. This task will be foreign to many students and they will need guidance in formulating the steps. Again, you can add significantly to this activity by sitting with each student and assisting in the development of the steps — particularly for those goals that pertain to school achievement.

When the students have completed both sections of the experience sheet break them into small groups. Tell the students to choose one of their stated goals to share with their group and explain the steps toward achievement they have identified. Allow for discussion and encourage the students to share the feelings and hopes they have associated with their goal.

Direct the students to keep their experience sheets and refer to them daily as they work toward their goals. Review the progress of the students regularly. Lead a discussion after each review using any of these and your own questions.

Discussion Questions:

1. How do you feel about having completed steps toward your goal?
2. If you haven't completed any steps, how do you feel about falling short? What can you do about it?
3. When you need the help of others to achieve a goal, how can you build in that requirement as part of your plan?
4. How disciplined do you have to be with yourself to keep working toward your goal?
5. How easy, or hard did you find it to keep focused on your goal?

You Can Reach Your Goals!
Experience Sheet

PART 1:

What are goals?
A goal is an end, home base, the final destination, what you are aiming for. Goals can center on having something —clothes, a car, money — or they can center on achieving — improving your grades, finishing school, going to college, having a career, becoming famous, gaining knowledge and honors.

Short-term and long-range goals:
Short-term goals include making phone calls, finishing your homework, cleaning your room, doing your chores, or making plans for the weekend. Long-range goals might include planning a trip for next summer, deciding to get a summer job, or saving money to buy something special.

Write down three of your goals.
Check whether each goal is short-term or long-range, and write in the date by which you plan to accomplish it. Try to come up with at least one long-term goal.

GOAL #1

_____
_____
_____
_____

___ Short Term   ___ Long Range
Target Date _____

GOAL #2

_____
_____
_____
_____

___ Short Term   ___ Long Range
Target Date _____

GOAL #3

_____
_____
_____
_____

___ Short Term   ___ Long Range
Target Date _____

PART 2:
Goal Achievement Score Sheet

GOAL #1 Steps Toward Achieving My Goal:	Review Date	Step Achieved	Step Not Achieved
1.			
2.			
3.			
4.			

GOAL #2 Steps Toward Achieving My Goal:	ReviewDate	Step Achieved	Step Not Achieved
1.			
2.			
3.			
4.			

GOAL #3 Steps Toward Achieving My Goal:	Review Date	Step Achieved	Step Not Achieved
1.			
2.			
3.			
4.			

Tips for Setting Goals
Experience Sheet

1. Goals must be clear and describe exactly what you want or will do.

2. Goals must be personal. They must be about you, not someone else.

3. Goals must be measurable. You need to know when you have achieved your goal.

4. Goals must have realistic time limits.

5. Goals must be manageable. Divide big goals into several smaller, attainable goals or tasks. This will enable you to experience results in a shorter period to time.

6. Goals must be stated in positive rather than negative terms: (I will do something rather than I won't do something.)

7. Goals should be written down. People are more likely to achieve goals that are in writing. Written goals can be reviewed regularly, and have more power. Like a contract with yourself, they are harder to neglect or forget.

Identifying Life Stressors
Self-Assessment and Discussion

Objectives: Students will:
—Describe the "fight or flight" response in their own words.
—Identify specific things that cause stress in their lives.
—Name activities that tend to reduce stress.

Materials: One copy of the experience sheet "What Causes Stress in Your Life?" for each student

Procedure: Explain to the students that what we call stress, and the feelings that accompany stress, are not only natural and normal, they have been experienced by every human being who has ever lived.

In your own words explain to the students: *Our earliest ancestors, the hunters and gatherers who lived long ago, evolved a very effective response to threats from predatory animals and other dangers. We call it the "fight or flight" response, because it helped them get ready to either stand and fight an attacker, or try to escape. When your heart pounds and your muscles get tense, when your eyes widen and your fists clench, you are experiencing almost exactly the same physical response. But, instead of worrying about hungry lions, you worry about tests, and grades, and peer pressure, and a busy schedule that sometimes leaves you exhausted. Your bloodstream is flooded with the same chemical brew that helped your ancestors survive terrible threats to their safety, but you don't really need all those chemicals. In fact, they can end up damaging your health. That is why it is so important to learn to manage stress. When you know how to calm down and relax, you can slow or stop the flow of chemicals before they do any damage.*

Point out that the first step to managing stress is to understand what causes the stress (fight or flight) response. Tell the students that they are going to complete a short self-assessment in order to identify sources of stress in their own lives.

Distribute the experience sheet, go over the directions, and allow time for completion.

When the students have completed their experience sheets read through the stress factors listed on the experience sheet, asking for a show of hands from the students who marked each item. After polling an item, ask volunteers to elaborate on their individual experiences. Make notes on the board to keep track of the most common sources of stress.

Next, talk to the students about the need to take breaks when they feel stressed. Explain that a break is anything that helps them relax and gets their mind off tough issues. Ask the students to describe the stress breaks they listed on their experience sheets. Write their ideas on the board under the heading "Stress Breaks." Then brainstorm additional strategies, including:
- Jog or walk
- Listen to music
- Spend time with your pet
- Work on a hobby
- Play a game
- Browse the Internet
- Watch TV or a movie
- Practice a musical instrument
- Dance
- Play sports
- Talk with a relative or friend
- Make a plan to solve the stressful problem

Emphasize that stress breaks give the students time to recover from the fight-or-flight response, so that their bodies don't continue to produce potentially damaging chemicals, and that this is the primary goal of all stress-management strategies.

Discussion Questions:
1. What is meant by the words fight-or-flight response?
2. What is the fight-or-flight response designed to accomplish?
3. Why is the same event stressful for one person, but not stressful for another?
4. What things do most of us in this group find stressful?
5. How does your body feel when you are stressed?
6. Why is it important to relieve stress? What can happen if we don't?

What Causes Stress in Your Life?
Experience Sheet

Read through the list. When you come to an area where you experience stress, write a short description of the thing that causes the stress. Remember two things:
A "change" in something can mean either more of it, or less of it. Both positive events and negative events can cause stress.

HEALTH
Personal injury or illness _____
Change in a family member's health _____
Change in personal-care habits _____
Change in sleep patterns _____
Change in eating habits _____
Change in exercise habits _____
Other _____

FRIENDS
Problems with friend(s) _____
Friend moving away _____
Problems with boyfriend/girlfriend _____
New friendship(s) _____
New boyfriend/girlfriend _____
Other _____

HOME
Change of address _____
Money problems at home _____
Pregnancy or new child in family _____
Change in living conditions _____
Change in home responsibilities _____
Brother/sister leaving home _____
Trouble with parent(s) _____
Parents separating/divorcing _____
Other _____

EXCITEMENT/ANTICIPATION
Outstanding personal achievement _____
Holiday season _____
Vacation _____
Other _____

SCHOOL
Starting new classes _____
Change in study hours or conditions _____
Change of school _____
Trouble with teacher(s) _____
New teacher(s) _____
Exams/tests _____
Report card _____
Other _____

ACTIVITIES
Change in number of family gatherings _____
Change in leisure hours/habits _____
Change in religious activities _____
Change in social activities _____
Other _____

DELINQUENCY
Expelled or suspended from school _____
Problems with alcohol/other drugs _____
Trouble with law _____
Other _____

DEATH
Death of a family member _____
Death of a friend _____
Death of a pet _____
Other _____

TAKE A STRESS BREAK
Three things I have done to relieve feelings of stress:

1. _____

2. _____

3. _____

Relaxation Three Ways
Deep Breathing, Meditation, and Muscle Relaxation

Objectives: Students will:
— Learn and practice three relaxation techniques.
— Understand the purpose of each technique.
— Compare the relative benefits of the three techniques.

Materials: reasonable space and moveable chairs; optional soft instrumental music

Procedure: The essence of stress reduction is relaxation. You can repeatedly urge mindfulness and relaxation, explaining in detail their value, but until you actually *teach* and *routinely practice* methods to accomplish these objectives — prior to tests, following breaks, as transitions from active to quiet tasks — nothing much will change.

Below are three distinct methods of achieving relaxation. Each is simple, easy to learn, and effective. The key to success is repetition. Have your students practice one or more of these exercises regularly. Make relaxation part of their routine.

Deep Breathing

The simplest, most direct route to relaxation is that of deep breathing. Explain to the students that when they are tense, nervous, angry, or excited, their breathing becomes more rapid. Deliberately slowing and controlling the depth and rate of their breathing can help them to calm down and feel more relaxed.

Have the students sit comfortably in their chairs and close their eyes while you lead them in this deep breathing exercise. Read the directions slowly so they can follow along with their breathing.

- *Slowly in hale through your nose to the count of four... 1... 2... 3... 4.*
- *Hold your breath to the count of four... 1... 2... 3... 4.*
- *Slowly exhale through your mouth to the count of four... 1... 2... 3... 4.*
- *Hold your breath to the count of four... 1... 2... 3... 4.*

Repeat several time.

Self-Management

5-Minute Meditation

Explain to the students that the purpose of meditation is to relax the body and quiet the mind. Point out that our bodies are usually active and moving. Even while sitting, we tend to shift, turn, and twitch. Similarly, our minds never stop producing thoughts, not even during sleep. By sitting quietly for a few minutes while breathing naturally and focusing all of our attention on one particular phrase, we can calm both mind and body.

In this exercise the students will focus on the phrase, "Breathe in calm, breathe out tension" as they breathe slowly and deeply in and out.

Read the directions slowly.
- *Sit straight in your chair. Fold your hands in your lap or rest them on your thighs.*
- *Close your eyes or look down slightly with your eyes, keeping your head straight.*
- *Sit quietly and try not to move. Breathe naturally.*

Pause briefly, then continue…

- *focus your attention on your breathing*
- *silently say "breathe in calm" as you slowly inhale.*
- *then silently say "breathe out tension" as you slowly exhale.*
- *continue breathing in and out as you concentrate on your words.*
- *"breathe in calm"… "breathe out tension".*
- *if other thoughts enter your mind that's okay. Just let them pass and go back to focusing on the phrase.*
- *"breathe in calm"… "breathe out tension".*

Continue sowly repeating the phrase *"breathe in calm"… "breathe out tension"* as the students follow along.

Progressive Muscle Relaxation

One of the best ways to differentiate a tense muscle from a relaxed one, thereby guaranteeing relaxation, is to first exaggerate the tension. Progressive muscle relaxation helps students feel the difference by tensing and relaxing one muscle group at a time, from toe to head. As you read the directions, exaggerate your inflexion to convey the alternate sensations of tension and relaxation. Play the role of coach.

Read the directions slowly.
- *Sit in a comfortable position with your eyes closed. Breathe naturally.*

- *Think about each set of muscles as I tell you to tense and hold for 5 seconds. Try to move only the muscles I tell you to move, keeping the rest of your body still. Notice how it feels. Then notice the difference when I tell you to relax those muscles.*
- *Tense your toes by flexing them as though you were standing on tiptoe. Hold... Relax.*
- *Flex your ankles and move them around in circles. Flex again. Hold... Relax.*
- *Tense and stretch your calf muscles by pushing hard with your heels. Hold... Relax.*
- *Tense the large muscles in your thighs. Hold... Relax.*
- *Tense your hip and buttocks muscles. Feel your hips lift. Hold... Relax.*
- *Tense your abdominal muscles. Feel them tighten. Hold... Relax.*
- *Tense your stomach muscles. Suck them in as tightly as you can. Hold... Relax.*
- *Make tight fists with your fingers. Tighter. Hold... Relax.*
- *Flex your wrists. Make circles with your wrists. Flex again. Hold... Relax.*
- *Tense the muscles in your arms. Make your arms as stiff as boards. Hold... Relax.*
- *Tense your shoulder muscles. Hunch your shoulders up to your ears. Hold... Relax.*
- *Tense your neck by touching your chin to your collarbone. Hold... Relax.*
- *Turn your neck as far as it will go to the right. Hold... Relax.*
- *Turn your neck as far as it will go to the left. Hold... Relax.*
- *Scrunch all the muscles of your face as tightly as you can. Hold... Relax.*
- *Now tense your whole body, starting with your toes all the way up to your face. Hold... Relax.*

Discussion Questions:

1. Which of the three relaxation exercises did you like best? Why?
2. Which exercise was most effective in helping you to relax?
3. Which exercise are you most apt to use on your own?
4. During the meditation, how difficult was it to concentrate on the phrase, "breathe in calm"... "breathe out tension"?
5. During the muscle relaxation exercise, where did you feel the most tension?
6. During what part of your day are you usually very relaxed? When are you usually very tense?
7. Which of these techniques could you use to relax during the tense part of your day?

Make Self-Talk Work For You
Discussion and Game

Objectives: The students will:
—state the importance of positive self-talk as an antidote to stress and upset
—describe the impact of self-talk on feelings and performance.

Materials: index cards listing stressful and upsetting situations (see directions, below)

Procedure: Introduce this activity by discussing the connection between stress, upset and anxiety and self-talk. Invite input from the students while making these points and offering examples:

- Responses to stressful and upsetting situations come from within.
- Self-talk (the words we say to ourselves) greatly effects how we feel, and what we believe, about ourselves and upsetting events.
- We engage in self-talk during most of our waking moments.
- Self-talk is like a conversation we have with ourselves, often about ourselves.
- Whether we feel better or worse in upsetting situations depends partly on what we say to ourselves.

To prepare for the game, think of a number of situations that commonly cause students to indulge in both positive and negative self-talk. Write the situations on index cards. (Use the situations listed below, add different situations based on your own observations, and ask the students to contribute others.)

Place the cards in a pile, face down.
Have a volunteer draw a card and read aloud the situation written on the card. Ask what the volunteer might say to himself or herself in that situation. For example, upon realizing that an important homework assignment has been left at home, a student might say, "I would forget my head if it weren't attached" or "The teacher's going to kill me."

Ask the class to decide if the statement represents negative or positive self-talk. You might call for a hand signal, such as "thumbs up" if the statement is positive or "thumbs down" if the statement is negative. If the statement is negative, give the student an opportunity to restate the response in positive terms. If the student has difficulty, ask the class to assist. For example, the student could say, "I forgot my homework today, but I am getting better at remembering my homework and other things. I have a good memory."

Continue until all of the cards have been drawn. Involve as many students as possible. Conduct a brief class discussion at the conclusion of the game.

Discussion Questions:

1. What differences did you notice between how you felt when your thoughts were positive and negative?
2. What do you find easiest about controlling self-talk? What do you find hardest?
3. What ideas do you have for getting control of your self-talk?
4. What impact do you think positive self-talk can have on your life? Negative self-talk?
5. How can understanding the benefits of positive self-talk help you use more of it in your life?
6. Does using positive self-talk require practice and commitment? Explain.

Situations:

- You forget to bring your homework to school.
- You get 4 out of 10 wrong on a spelling test.
- You get 9 out of 10 right on a quiz.
- You miss the school bus.
- You weren't chosen for the team.
- You strike out in a softball game.
- You move to a new neighborhood.
- Your best friend goes shopping with someone else.
- You arrive late to class.
- You get an A on an assignment.
- A group project goes well.
- Your new haircut didn't turn out like you wanted it to.
- You spill your milk at lunch.
- You have a library book that is six weeks overdue.
- You run for student council and lose.
- You run for student council and win.
- Someone points out that you have a stain on your shirt.
- You have to complete a lengthy report on the civil war.
- You get a B- on your book report.
- You are asked to baby-sit.

Control Yourself!
Discussion and Pantomine

Objectives: The students will:
—identify different kinds of self-control and self-management,
—demonstrate behaviors associated with self-control in a variety of situations
—publicly affirm how they feel about their own levels of self-control.

Procedure: Begin this session by asking the students what the term self-control means. Listen to and reflect the students' responses. In the process, establish that having self-control means being able to restrain and regulate one's own behavior. Then say: Think of a time when your emotions were so strong that you couldn't control yourself. Maybe you didn't want to cry or yell or laugh, but the feelings were overpowering.

Invite volunteers to tell the class about their experiences. Ask for volunteers to act out their incidents, demonstrating exactly what happened.

Next, whisper one of the following situations to a volunteer and have that student act out the situation in pantomime (nonverbally). Have the class guess what is happening and identify the emotion that the student is trying to control.

- You just crashed your bike, banging your leg badly, in front of several older kids.
- You get back a paper that you worked very hard on. It's covered with red marks and graded C-.
- Walking home at dusk, you turn a corner and practically run right into a big skunk.
- While your teacher is explaining an assignment, you see another student do something hysterically funny and try to keep from breaking up.
- Your parent restricts you for something your brother or sister did.
- You are walking home alone after just learning that a boy or girl you have a crush on likes you, too.

Repeat this process with the remainder of the situations and a new volunteer each time. After each pantomime, talk about methods typically used to control reactions to various emotions (biting tongue, clenching fists, taking deep breaths, blinking, stiffening muscles, looking away, etc.)

Draw a long horizontal line across the board. At one end write "Volcanic Vicki." At the other end write, "Restrained Robert." Explain to the students that the line is a self-control continuum and that Vicki and Robert represent the extreme endpoints. Ask the students to help you describe Vicki and Robert. Have fun with this and encourage the students to exaggerate their descriptions. For example:

Volcanic Vicki is going off all the time. At the slightest provocation, steam spews from her nostrils, tears from her eyes, and agonizing, earth shaking sounds from her throat. Vicki was once able to control herself for 20 seconds, and that was when a bee landed on her nose.

Restrained Robert looks a little like an automated store mannequin. His expression almost never changes and his movements are stiff and controlled. People have exhausted themselves trying to make Robert laugh, or blink, or get angry. But Robert would rather die than lose control.

Ask two or three students at a time to write their names somewhere on the continuum. Explain that before they do this, they must decide how much self-control they have. Are they closer to Vicki's end of the continuum or Robert's? Give all of the students an opportunity to place themselves on the line.

Lead a culminating class discussion, focusing on the concepts of self-control and self-management. Then, with the last few minutes remaining, play a little game with the students. Tell them to sit absolutely still, without fidgeting, talking, or blinking. Explain that the last student to move is the winner. Time the students and proclaim the winner, "Self-control King" or "Self-control Queen" for the day.

Discussion Questions:
1. Why is it important to learn self-control?
2. What would school be like if students and teachers never made any effort to manage their feelings or behavior?
3. What does self-management have to do with responsibility?
4. What do your parents mean when they tell you to "be on your best behavior?"
5. How do you feel when you successfully control yourself?

A Time I Handled My Feelings Well
A Sharing Circle

Objectives: The students will:
—identify ways to express and deal with feelings.
—demonstrate a positive attitude about self.

Introduce the Topic. In your own words say to the students: *We all face situations that cause us to experience strong feelings. How we behave at those times depends on how well we take charge of our feelings. Today, we're going to talk about instances when the outcome was good. Our topic is, "A Time I Handled My Feelings Well."*

For example, maybe you wanted a special gift for your birthday or Christmas and didn't receive it because your parents either failed to realize how important it was to you or couldn't afford it. Since you didn't want to hurt their feelings, you didn't express your disappointment to them, but told a friend instead. Perhaps you were very angry at someone and wanted to hit the person, but instead managed to talk to him or her and express your angry feelings without hitting. Maybe you lost a game or an election and really wanted to yell, but instead congratulated the winner. Possibly you injured yourself and it hurt so badly that you needed to cry, so you did. Handling your feelings well usually means doing what is appropriate, without hurting someone else in the process. Think of a situation that you feel okay sharing. When you are ready, raise your hand. The topic is, "A Time I Handled My Feelings Well."

Discussion Questions:
1. What similarities were there in the ways we handled our feelings? What differences were there?
2. If our feelings are always acceptable, why isn't our behavior always acceptable?
3. What do we have to control, our feelings or our behavior? How can we do that?

A Secret Fear I Have
A Sharing Circle

Objectives: The students will:
—describe fears that they usually keep to themselves.
—discuss ways in which fears can be managed.

Introduce the Topic: In your own words say to the students: *The topic of today's Sharing Circle is, "A Secret Fear I Have." A secret is something no one else knows about. Fear is an emotion that causes us distress, anxiety, or a sense of dread. All of us probably harbor secrets about ourselves, things we don't want anyone else to know. Perhaps we keep such things to ourselves because we think people won't like or accept us if they know; we are afraid they might laugh or make fun of us. Just as we all have secrets, we also have fears. Everyone is afraid of something. You may fear the dark, lightening and thunder, or strange dogs. You may have a fear of flying or being in high places. You may fear getting lost, being alone, swimming in deep water, or some other situation or thing. Think for a moment about a secret fear you have and are willing to share with us. Our topic is, "A Secret Fear I Have."*

Discussion Questions:
1. What is something that we all have in common, based on what we shared?
2. How did it feel to share a secret? How do you feel now after taking that risk?
3. What have you learned about yourself from thinking or sharing on this topic?
4. What steps can we take to overcome our fears, or handle them better?

Self-Management

Something I Do for My Own Well-Being
A Sharing Circle

Objectives: The students will:
—describe a way they manage stress.
—discuss the importance of taking responsibility for one's own well-being.

Introduce the Topic: In your own wards say to the students: *Our topic for this circle session is a very useful one because it gives us a chance to talk about things we do that help us get rid of stress and enjoy life. It's also going to allow us to pick up some good tips from each other on how to be our own best friend. The topic is, "Something I Do for My Own Well-Being."*

Most of us find ways to be good to ourselves, but with all the stress each one of us has to deal with, the more ideas we can get for managing stress, the better. Think about things you do for yourself to be healthy, to relax, play, or feel good in general. Perhaps you have a special time when you go off alone to think calmly and take in pleasant surroundings. Maybe you have a form of exercise you do that helps you get rid of tension and allows you to rest very well afterward. You may enjoy losing yourself in some kind of creative activity that relieves built-up stress. Whatever it is, we'd enjoy hearing about it. The topic is, "Something I Do for My Own Well-Being."

Discussion Questions:
1. Who has the most influence on how well or how poorly you manage your stress levels?
2. What similarities did you notice in the methods that were mentioned?
3. What new ideas did you get for managing stress?

I Stood Up for Something I Strongly Believe In
A Sharing Circle

Objectives: The students will:
—describe times when they behaved assertively regarding a strongly held value or principle.
—demonstrate an understanding of assertive versus nonassertive behaviors.

Introduce the Topic: In your own words say to the students: *Many times during our lives, we are given the opportunity to speak out for the things we believe in. Taking a stand can be a difficult experience, especially if friends or relatives don't agree with our position. Even when they do agree, it's not necessarily easy to state our beliefs publicly. Today, we're going to talk about the conviction and determination these situations demand. Our topic is, "I Stood Up for Something I Strongly Believe In."*

Perhaps you saw a group of people doing something that you felt was wrong. Maybe you observed some kids teasing or harassing another kid, and intervened. Or maybe, during a conversation about a controversial subject, you stated your beliefs even though everyone else in the group held the opposing view. If you decide to share, please don't mention the names of the other people involved. The topic is, "I Stood Up for Something I Strongly Believe In."

Discussion Questions:
1. As you look back on the situation you shared, how do you feel about it right now?
2. Why is it sometimes hard to stand up for your beliefs?
3. What are the risks and benefits of taking a stand?
4. What are some ills in our society that people need to take a stand against?

Something I Enjoy Doing Because It Gives Me a Feeling of Accomplishment

A Sharing Circle

Objective: The students will describe personal accomplishments and the feelings they generate.

Introduce the Topic: In your own words say to the students: *Today we're going to discuss things we're good at. The topic is, "Something I Enjoy Doing Because It Gives Me a Feeling of Accomplishment." Notice that you're asked to brag a little here, and that's OK. You aren't boasting, and you're not comparing yourself to others or putting anyone else down. You're just telling about what you can do that you're proud of. So think about one thing you like to do that gives you a good feeling. This can be something you enjoy doing at school or away from school. It can be something you've only done once, or an activity you engage in frequently. Think about it for a minute. The topic is, "Something I Enjoy Doing Because It Gives Me A Feeling of Accomplishment."*

Discussion Questions:
1. What is it about the activity you shared that gives you such good feelings?
2. How important is it to experience feelings of accomplishment?
3. Did you learn anything new and interesting about anyone in this session?
4. What did you learn about yourself?

One of My Best Habits
A Sharing Circle

Objective: The students will identify and describe positive habits they have developed.

Introduce the topic: In your own words say to the students: *In our circle today, we're going to talk about good habits we've developed. The topic is, "One of My Best Habits." What good habits do you have? Maybe you do something every single day for your health, like brush your teeth. Or maybe you have the good habit of always making sure you are on time for school and other places you are supposed to be. Perhaps you make it a habit to do things to keep your life organized and smooth-running, like putting your things where they belong at home. Tell us about any good habit that you have developed. Let's think about it for a moment. Then, when you are ready to share, raise your hand. The topic is, "One of My Best Habits."*

Discussion Questions:
1. How do good habits cause us to feel about ourselves?
2. Did you get any ideas for good habits you'd like to start developing in yourself?
3. You don't have to tell us what it is, but did you realize that you might have a bad habit or two that you'd like to change?

Social Awareness

We All Have Talents
Writing, Sharing, and Discussion

Objectives: The students will:
—describe their unique abilities and talents.
—acknowledge the abilities and talents of classmates.
—demonstrate understanding of the concept, "strength in diversity."

Materials: one copy of the experience sheet, "My Special Gifts and Talents," and writing materials for each student

Procedure: Introduce the activity by asking the students to think about talents or "gifts" that they possess. Explain that a talent or gift is a special ability, like the ability to play a musical instrument or to draw pictures, or speak another language. Some people have a talent for math, science, or history; others are gifted at making friends or playing a particular sport. A gift or talent can be almost anything a person does well. Describe to the students two or three gifts or talents that you possess.

Distribute the experience sheet, "My Special Gifts and Talents." Have the students record their name at the top of the sheet, and then write down as many of their own gifts/talents as they can think of. While the students are working, circulate and offer help and suggestions as needed. Ensure that every student identifies and records several gifts/talents.

When they have completed their experience sheets, ask the students to look over what they have written, and to circle one talent that they would feel comfortable describing to their classmates. Then have the students form groups of four to six, and take turns sharing their thoughts and feelings about their identified talent. Conclude with a general discussion helping the students to reflect on the value of diversity in all things.

Discussion Questions:

1. What is a gift or talent? How can you recognize your own talents?
2. How are our gifts and talents the same? How are they different?
3. What would the world be like if everyone had exactly the same gifts and talents?
4. What would happen if everyone on a football team were a talented passer, but no one had a talent for blocking, kicking, catching, running, or calling plays?
5. Explain what the term "strength in diversity" means to you.
6. How can we use our individual talents and abilities to make our class a better place to learn?
7. What are other differences we each bring to this group?
8. How do we benefit from diversity of all kinds?

My Special Gifts and Talents
Experience Sheet

Everyone has things they can do well. These are probably not things you think about everyday, but your abilities are many. Recall some of the things you do, and do well. They can be big or little and in any area of life. Write down some of them here.

I, _____ , bring these special gifts and talents to my classroom:

1. _____
   _____

2. _____
   _____

3. _____
   _____

4. _____
   _____

5. _____
   _____

6. _____
   _____

7. _____
   _____

How Do They Feel?
Pantomime and Discussion

Objectives: The students will:
—demonstrate nonverbal behaviors appropriate to specific feelings.
—correctly identify feelings based on body language, facial expressions, and other nonverbal cues.
—recognize that feelings are conveyed primarily through nonverbal means.

Materials: descriptions of situations written on small pieces of paper, folded and placed in a container — one description for every two students. Suggested situations are written on the next page. If you use those situations photocopy the page and cut along the dotted line. If you choose to write your own situations they should portray a variety of emotion-producing situations.

Procedure: Ask the students to pair up. Have each pair draw one sheet of paper with a situation written on it. Direct each pair to go off to a private place for five minutes and plan a short pantomime of the situation. Explain that the students are to act only with their faces and bodies. They may neither say words, nor make vocal noises. The object is to do such a good job of acting that the class will be able to tell how each actor is feeling in his or her role. This is similar to a game of Charades. If the class can guess the situation, that's fine, but it is not necessary. The objective is to identify the feelings being portrayed.

When the students have finished planning, have them enact their pantomimes one pair at a time. Enjoy each pantomime and applaud when it is over.

After each pantomime, ask the class to tell the actors how they appeared to be feeling in their roles. Finally, ask the actors to describe the situation they were acting out and the feelings they tried to convey.

When all the situations have been portrayed and discussed lead a summary discussion with the entire group using these and any of your own questions.

Discussion Questions:

1. Do our bodies and faces have a language of their own?
2. What did you learn about language through this activity?
3. How much empathy did you feel for the actors? What enabled you to feel empathy?
4. How do people reveal their emotions — mostly through their words or mostly through their facial expressions and body language?
5. If you want to really empathize with someone, what should you pay close attention to?
6. What clues can you look for to understand how another person is feeling?
7. Can you think of a time when someone knew how you were feeling without you telling them? How do you think they knew?

Situations:

- You just got a new puppy and your friend is very jealous.
- You and your friend are walking down a dark street at night. Suddenly, you hear a strange noise, but your friend doesn't hear it and thinks you are making it up.
- You and your friend are competing for first place in the tennis tournament. Your friend wins and is elated, but you feel disappointed.
- Your friend borrowed your bike and brought it back with a dent in the fender. You're angry and blame your friend for the dent. Your friend thinks the dent was already there and is upset because you blame them.
- Your friend is trying to get you to do something that you know is wrong. Your friend is being assertive in trying to convince you to do it. You're giving a very clear message of "No Way".
- You were supposed to meet your friend at 3pm but you got distracted and arrived half an hour late. Your friend is upset, and you're trying to calm your friend down.
- You're talking with a classmate when they start saying very negative, untrue things about one of your friends. You're trying to tell the classmate that what they are saying isn't true and you want them to stop saying those things. The classmate just keeps it up not listening to your comments.
- Your parent won't let you go to a party with your friends because they think it will be wild and unruly. You're trying to convince your parent that you'll be safe and careful. Your parent isn't buying what you are saying.

How Would You Feel? Part 1
A Group Discussion

Objectives: The students will:
—identify social problems common to young people.
—associate typical situations with emotional responses.
—describe ways of resolving typical social problems.

Procedure: Read the following situations to the students, one at a time. Ask the questions listed and discuss each situation before going on to the next.

Note: In place of the following situations, you may substitute examples that are more relevant to problems occurring right now in your own school. However, should the group members know any of the students involved, do not allow them to mention names.

- Sandra's family doesn't have much money and she wears clothes that are old and out of style. She can't seem to make friends with the other girls in class. They ignore her and don't include her in any of their activities.
—What is Sandra's problem?
—How do you think Sandra feels?
—How would you feel if you were in a similar situation?
—Can Sandra do anything about her clothes?
—If you were in the class, how would you treat Sandra?

- Manny has been called into the principal's office for fighting. In the past, Manny has been a quiet student, but this year the kids are calling him names like "Fat Man," "Lard Face," and "The Whale."
—What is Manny's problem?
—How do you think Manny feels?
—How would you feel if you were in a similar situation?
—If you were in the class and were Manny's friend, what would you do?
—What do you think Manny should do?

- Off and on for several weeks, Lisa has been finding excuses not to dress for physical education class. First it's a cold, then a sore shoulder, and now a sprained ankle wrapped with an ace bandage. The P.E. teacher finally sends Lisa to talk with the counselor. Later that day, the counselor tells the teacher that Lisa is upset because several girls in class make fun of her appearance and lack of coordination. Sometimes the same girls are rude, push her, or call her "retard."
—What is Lisa's problem?
—How do you think Lisa feels?
—How would you feel if you were in a similar situation?
—If you were in the class and were Lisa's friend, what would you do?
—What do you think Lisa should do?

- Kevin is 12 years old. He is taller than the other boys his age, and his voice is beginning to change. One day, while giving a report in class, his voice suddenly drops and he lets out a couple of loud croaking sounds while trying to regain control of his speech. Everyone in class breaks out laughing. Even after the teacher quiets the students, they quietly giggle and snicker. No one listens to the rest of Kevin's report.
—What is Kevin's problem?
—How do you think Kevin feels?
—How would you feel if you were in a similar situation?
—If you were in the class and were Kevin's friend, what would you do?

When you have finished talking about the four example problems, move the discussion to real problems with which the students are dealing.

Discussion Questions:

1. Have you ever had a problem similar to any of the ones we talked about? If so, would you be willing to talk about it?
2. How do problems like this affect the self-concept of the person it's happening to?
3. Why do some students tease and harass other students?
4. Do you think students are more apt to tease and torment when they are alone or part of a group? Why?
5. How does it make you feel when you see, or hear about, someone being treated like this?
6. What could you do to get someone else to stop harassing you?
7. What can you do to help someone else who is being harassed?

How Would You Feel? Part 2
Experience Sheet and Discussion

Objectives: The students will:
—examine racial/cultural issues.
—describe feelings related to racial issues

Materials: one copy of the experience sheet, "Put Yourself in This Situation" for each student

Procedure: Distribute the experience sheets. Give the students time to fill them out. If you want to encourage longer, more thoughtful responses, ask the students to complete them as homework.

Note: Allow the students to approach the questions in any way they choose. Some of the questions are worded so that they may represent the view of either a minority or a majority person. This ambiguity could add interest to the discussion.

When the students have completed their questionnaire ask which question they want to discuss first. Give students who are particularly troubled or confused by an item the opportunity to air their concerns. Encourage the sharing of personal experiences similar to those described.

One at a time, discuss each situation on the Experience Sheet questionnaire. As each item is discussed, ask the questions listed below along with other relevant open-ended questions. If your group is large have the students share their responses first in small groups of three or four, so that all students get to share their feelings. Ask those who would like to share with the entire group to do so.

Discussion Questions:
1. What is really going on in this situation?
2. What would your very first feelings be in this situation? What about later?
3. What do you think you would say or do in this situation?
5. What, if anything, would you like to see done about this kind of situation? What are you willing to do?

Put Yourself in This Situation
Experience Sheet

Describe how you would feel in each of these situations:
How would you feel if...

- You had to pay "up front" before being served at a restaurant?

- The fences and walls in your once nice neighborhood were being covered with graffiti?

- You'd been waiting in a long line and when it was your turn, the clerk ignored you and went on to the next person?

- Your little brother/sister didn't understand the social slights and racial slurs of other kids, and you had to explain them to him/her?

- You were never invited when your friends went swimming at a private club?

- Women visibly clutched their handbags tighter when you passed them on the street?

- You were stopped for no apparent reason — other than your appearance — and asked to prove your legal residency?

- People were always getting impatient — even angry — with you because of your heavy accent in English?

Don't Destroy Enthusiasm
Brainstorming and Role Playing

Objectives: The students will:
—brainstorm and list statements that can damage a person's feelings, ideas, and enthusiasm, as well as block communication.
—demonstrate alternative positive statements.
—describe methods of improving communication behaviors in themselves and others.

Materials: whiteboard

Procedure: Facilitate a discussion about appropriate and inappropriate ways to respond to another person's ideas, accomplishments, feelings, etc. In your own words, say: *Have you ever come up with a great idea that you couldn't wait to share with someone? But when you described your idea, the person you told made fun of it, or put you down in some way? Have you been afraid to share your strong feelings about something because you were certain no one would understand or, worse, you'd be ridiculed for your feelings? We can easily destroy a person's enthusiasm just by the things we say. We may not mean to do it, but we can kill their ideas and make them feel foolish for feeling the way they do.*

Write the heading "**Destroyer Statements**" on the board.

Ask the students to help you brainstorm a list of statements that can hurt communication and damage the feelings, ideas, and enthusiasm of others. Write their ideas on the board under the heading. Include statements such as:
- Can't you see I'm busy?
- Are you kidding me?
- You can't be serious!
- What a stupid idea!
- Just like a guy.
- That's a silly question.
- You shouldn't feel that way.
- Don't be such a wimp.
- Who asked for your opinion?
- Not bad for a girl.

Social Awareness

Have pairs of volunteers role play some of the items from the list. Instruct one person to initiate an interaction and the other to respond using the "destroyer" statement. After each role play, ask the actors to describe their thoughts and feelings during the exchange. Then have the group think of at least three alternative positive responses that could be used in that situation. Role play and debrief those as well.

Facilitate a summary discussion.

Discussion Questions:

1. Why do we respond to others with put-downs and other types of destroyer statements?
2. Where do you think we learn this type of communication?
3. If you know someone who frequently makes these kinds of statements to you and others, what can you do about it?
4. How can you change your own bad communication habits?

Extend the Learning:

Have the students observe and record all of the destroyer statements they hear at school, home, on TV and elsewhere for the next week. Set a time to discuss their findings.

Thumbprint Mural
Art Activity and Discussion

Objectives: The students will:
—describe differences among people.
—examine and compare their thumbprints.
—identify and appreciate some of their own differences.

Materials: large sheet of butcher paper or newsprint, masking tape, colored markers, ink pad

Procedure: Tape the butcher paper or newsprint to a board or wall. Set out the ink pad and marking pens.

Announce to the group that the subject of this session is differences among people. Ask the students to think of all the ways in which they are different from one another. They will probably mention such things as hair, eye and skin color; facial features; names and birth dates; family differences; interests and abilities; etc.

If no one mentions fingerprints, point out that the uniqueness of fingerprints has made them a primary means of identifying one person from another.

Tell the students that they are going to have an opportunity to compare thumbprints. Press your own thumb to the ink pad and stamp your thumbprint on the butcher paper. Then, pick two or more colored markers and write your name and something unique about yourself in a circle, wavy line, or other pattern around the thumbprint. For example, you might write:

Ms. Patterson — makes the best spaghetti sauce in town.

One at a time, invite the students to add their thumbprints and statements to the mural. Ask them to read their statements aloud so that everyone can hear them.

Give the group an opportunity to closely examine the completed mural, noting the differences in thumbprints. Lead a culminating discussion.

Discussion Questions:
1. What makes our thumbprints different from one another?
2. How are our thumbprints alike?
3. Can you tell a person's religion or the color of his/her skin from a thumbprint? Why not?
4. Out of all the differences among people, why do you think such a big deal is made out of things like skin color, religion and ethnic background?
5. What did you learn about someone in the group that you didn't know before?
6. What did you learn from this activity?

The Problem With Stereotypes
Brainstorming and Discussion

Objectives: The students will:
—define the term stereotype.
—identify common stereotypes based on race.
—describe problems caused by stereotyping.
—suggest ways of reducing or eliminating harmful stereotypes at school.

Materials: whiteboard

Procedure: Begin by asking the students to help you list different racial groups represented in the school. As each group is identified, write it as a heading on the board.

Next, define the word stereotype. Give the students plenty of time to debate/discuss various ideas. If they need help, here is one possible definition:

An oversimplified opinion or mental picture held in common by members of a group. (Stereotypes are different from racism, which is always negative and assumes that some races are better than others.)

When the students have a good grasp of the concept, engage them in brainstorming a list of stereotypes for each of the racial groups listed. In your own words, ask: *What oversimplified ideas and opinions do we have of each other based on race? What have you heard adults or kids say, seen on TV, or social media, or learned through jokes, music, or movies?*

Encourage the students to be candid by setting a matter-of-fact, non-judgmental tone. Depending on the age, sophistication, and trust level of the group, you may generate items such as:

Whites
 self-centered; anti-family
 only care about money
 violent; worship violent heroes
 racist

Social Awareness

Latinos
    poor
    lazy; don't want to study or work
    don't treat women equally
    have too many children

Blacks
    athletic
    drug users and dealers
    violent
    less intelligent

Asians
    smart; best students
    meek; unassertive
    unathletic
    form cliques; exclude others

Next, ask the students: Which stereotypes do you think exist widely at our school? Which ones are interfering with our ability to show everyone equal respect and include all students equally in activities?

Go through the lists and check off those items that the students think are causing problems.

Have the students work in teams of three or four. Instruct them to take only those stereotypes that were checked and rank them from "most harmful" to "least harmful." Then have the teams discuss ways of reducing or eliminating the top two on their ordered lists.

Allow the teams to work for about 15 minutes. Then have them present their rankings to the rest of the group along with their ideas for eliminating or reducing the most serious stereotyping. Lead a culminating discussion.

Discussion Questions:

1. Why do groups stereotype each other?
2. How do stereotypes get started? How do they stay alive?
3. How do stereotypes hurt individuals… all members of the group being stereotyped?
4. How can stereotypes lead to racism?
5. How can we keep from making assumptions about people we don't know?
6. What can you do personally to eliminate stereotyping here at school? …at home?

Recognizing the Needs of Others
Experience Sheets and Discussion

Objectives: The students will:
—understand the importance of empathy and how empathy is achieved.
—empathize with people in a variety of situations.

Materials: one copy of the experience sheets, "Empathy Is..." and "Empathy Practice," for each student

Procedure: Give a copy of the experience sheet, "Empathy Is...," to each student. Tell the students that they have 3 minutes to translate the Braille sentence at the top of the sheet. Call time and have the students stop working. Ask:
— *Did anyone complete the translation? If so, what does the sentence say?*

Call on volunteers to read their translations, If no one was able to translate the sentence in the allotted time (which is likely), acknowledge the difficulty of the task and write the correct translation on the board. (Translation: *Empathy is imagining yourself in another person's shoes and feeling what they feel.*)

Have the students write the correct translation in the space provided on the bottom of the experience sheet. Ask:
—*How did you feel when you could not easily understand what you were reading?*

Encourage sharing. The point being to get the students to get in touch with their feelings and then to transpose those feelings to how others might feel in situations where they are unsure.

Call on volunteers. Discuss the similarity between the situation they faced with the Braille and the experience of a student who must adjust to a new culture with an unfamiliar language, or a student with a disability learning to perform a difficult skill. Ask:
—*Did this experience help you empathize with the student who can't speak English, or the student who is physically challenged by a disability?*

Social Awareness

Talk about what it means to empathize with another person. Differentiate empathy from sympathy. Empathy is not feeling sorry for someone. Empathy is identifying with the person, feeling what they feel. For most people, empathy is not a well-developed response. Sometimes it requires conscious thought. Explain that they may have to ask themselves, "What is this person feeling right now?" and "How would I feel in their situation?"

Read the Empathy Situations below to the students. After each one, ask the listed questions and call on volunteers to name their projected feelings. Write these on the board. Use their answers to generate discussion. For example, if a student says he would feel protective and angry as the parent of the immigrant child (first situation), ask "Why?" or "What thoughts led you to that conclusion?" Encourage the students to put themselves in the shoes of the various people—to really "get inside" their heads and hearts.

Empathy Situations

1. Luce is a new student at your school. She dresses differently from the other girls. Her clothes fit poorly and are not stylish. When the kids make fun of her and call her names, Luce tells her parents. Her father visits the school to find out what is going on. How would you feel if you were 1) Luce, 2) Luce's father, 3) the school principal?

2. Marcie Brown and her children buy a house on a large lot next to a big apartment complex. They discover that the apartments' drainage ditch crosses the back of their property. They want the drainage ditch moved so that they can build a pool, but the city says that the apartment complex can keep their drainage ditch where it is because it was built when their property was just an empty lot, giving the apartment complex what is called a "prescriptive easement." How would you feel if you were 1) Marcie Brown, 2) the owner of the apartment complex, 3) Marcie Brown's kids (who probably won't get a pool)?

3. Your city plans to demolish several blocks of old hotels and low-income apartment houses to build a new baseball stadium. Several hundred people will lose their homes. While the owners of the buildings will be paid by the city, the renters won't get anything. They band together and try to

stop the city from building the ballpark. How would you feel if you were 1) a renter in danger of losing your home, 2) the owner of one of the condemned buildings, 3) the developer of the baseball stadium, 4) the city mayor, 5) a baseball fan?

4. Kim and Tracey have been best friends for years. One day Susan moves in next door to Kim and the two girls quickly become inseparable. Tracey tries to make it a threesome, but finds herself left out much of the time. How would you feel if you were 1) Tracey, 2) Kim, 3) Susan?

5. Jermane spends hours in the library researching the Lewis and Clark expedition for a written report. He gets a B. His friend Donovan downloads a report from the Internet and gets an A. Jermane complains to his mom who, against Jermane's wishes, tells the teacher. How would you feel if you were 1) Jermane, 2) Jermane's mother, 3) the teacher, 4) Donovan?

Give a copy of the experience sheet, "Empathy Practice," to each student. Go over the directions. Announce that for one week, you want them to watch and listen for feelings. Point out that feelings are a lot more difficult to notice than physical things like how someone looks. Suggest that the students be alert for situations that involve some sort of problem or conflict, like the ones you read to them earlier.

When the students bring in their completed sheets, have them take turns reporting what they observed. Go around the group and discuss one situation from each student. Then repeat the circuit as time allows.

Culminate the activity by asking these and your own questions to help the students reflect on their learning.

Discussion Questions:

1. What is the most difficult thing about being empathetic?
2. What kinds of feelings were easier to discern, positive feelings or negative feelings? Why do you think that is?
3. Why is having empathy important?
4. Would you rather have friends who empathize with what you feel, or friends who don't seem to notice? Explain?

Empathy Is...
Experience Sheet

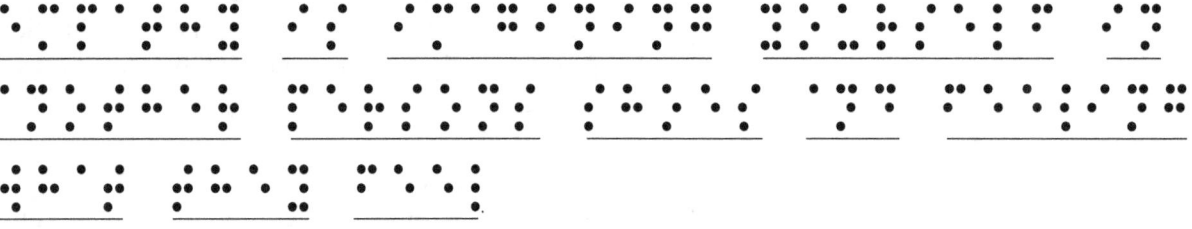

Using the Braille alphabet above, translate the following sentence. (Each word is separately underlined.)

Write your translation here:

_____

_____

_____

_____

_____

_____

Empathy Practice
Experience Sheet

For one week, notice situations in which people have strong feelings. Write down what was going on. Then try to empathize with each of the people involved. Write down what you think they feel.

Situation:	Feelings:

Showing Care and Concern for Others

Dramatizations and Discussion

Objectives: The students will:
—discuss ways of demonstrating empathy and caring.
—practice empathic, caring behaviors in a variety of dramatized scenarios.

Materials: whiteboard; found materials for props (optional)

Procedure: Explain to the students that there are many ways to demonstrate empathy and caring. Ask the students to think about ways in which they can show care and concern for other people. Generate a list of words and phrases that describe ways of caring and write them on the board. Here are some suggestions:

- listening
- cheering up someone
- helping
- volunteering
- inviting someone to do something with you
- sharing
- smiling
- acknowledging feelings
- thanking
- greeting new students
- accompanying
- hugging
- shaking hands
- thinking about your actions and their consequences
- treating others fairly
- giving presents
- singing to someone
- writing to a friend.

Discuss possible role-play situations using one of the words or phrases on the list. For example, the word volunteering could generate these scenarios:

- A teacher introduces a new student and asks if someone would show her around the school and help her set up her locker. A student raises his hand to volunteer and does the job.

- A kid, noticing that mom is very tired from working all day, volunteers to set the table for dinner and clear the table afterwards.

Discuss the possible actions and dialogue that might take place in each scenario. Then model the role-playing process by choosing volunteers to act out each scenario.

Divide the class into small groups and have each group choose one of the words from the board. Tell the groups to develop two or three scenarios that, when acted out, will effectively demonstrate that caring behavior. Have them assign a group member to each role, and then practice the scenario, making sure that every person has at least one part to play. Ask the students to repeat this procedure for each scenario they develop.

When the groups are finished practicing, invite them to dramatize their scenarios for the rest of the class. After each group is finished, discuss that group's dramatizations before going on to the next group. Ask, *How did these situations demonstrate the value of caring?*

Following all of the dramatizations, facilitate a culminating discussion.

Discussion Questions:
1. How do you know how another person feels?
2. What are clues you can look for to try to understand how another person is feeling?
3. Did feeling empathy for the other person in your scenario help you decide how to show caring?
4. What is empathy and how do you know when you've got it?
5. How do you know when a behavior shows caring?
6. What would life be like if no one cared about you? ...if you cared about no one?
7. Is it possible to care about people we don't know? Explain.

Speaking Out Against Bullying
Brainstorming and Discussion

Objectives: The students will:
—Identify interventions they can make to stop bullying and hurtful behavior.
—Recognize that maintaining a peaceful, respectful school climate is everyone's responsibility.

Materials: one copy of the experience sheet, "Stop Bullying! It's Everyone's Responsibility!," for each student

Procedure: Point out that incidents of bullying and hurtful behavior that happen at school often occur in busy places, like hallways, lunch areas, in front of the school and on playgrounds. Although adults don't usually see these things happen, very often other kids are nearby and do witness the incidents, but don't know what to do.

Ask the students to help you brainstorm things that witnesses can do to stop students from bullying one another. Add the following four ideas if they are not mentioned by the group.

1. Confront the person who is bullying. Say something like, "Leave Sally alone. It's wrong to talk mean to others."
2. If the hurtful person is just showing off, don't give him or her an audience. Walk away.
3. If appropriate and safe, distract the kids involved.
4. Create safety in numbers. If you know that a particular student is often harassed, put down, bullied or treated meanly, make sure that the victim is not alone in places where he or she is vulnerable.
5. Report fights and other violent acts.

Write the following headings on the board:
Who   **How**

Stress that students should talk to an adult about every incident of bullying or violence that occurs. Under the "Who" heading, list appropriate adults.

Discuss ways of reporting that guard the safety of students, such as writing an anonymous note, going to the office after school when the rest of the kids have gone home, or calling a teacher or counselor at home. List these ideas under "How." Make a distinction between tattling and snitching and reporting an incident. Tattling is about wanting to get someone in trouble. Informing an adult is about wanting to help the victim.

Distribute the experience sheets and go over the directions. After allowing the students time to complete the sheet, ask volunteers to read their top five ideas. Facilitate discussion. Try to honor and implement ideas that seem workable, developing action plans, as needed.

Discussion Questions:

1. Why do people bully and say and do hurtful things to one another?
2. What would you do if you saw your best friend being hurtful to someone?
3. What would you do if you saw a student you didn't know bullying someone?
4. When you feel angry at someone, what can you do to avoid being mean or disrespectful?
5. How can we have a peaceful school where everyone respects everyone else?

Stop Bullying!
It's Everyone's Responsibility
Experience Sheet

It is up to everyone in the school to stop hurtful, bullying behavior. When you and other students decide that it is time to stand up to kids who try to hurt others, you can really make a difference. When you mobilize and take action, you can help put an end to bullying. Wouldn't you like to have a caring, peaceful school?

What can be done to stop kids from harassing each other? List your ideas here:

_____
_____
_____
_____
_____

What can **YOU** do?

_____
_____
_____
_____

Cross out any ideas that involve violence or retaliation. Don't ever do what you want the other person to stop doing. Besides, violence usually makes things worse.

Go back and look at each of your ideas. Ask yourself, "Will this idea really work?" Cross out any ideas that simply will not work.

Now, pick your five best ideas and number them #1 to #5. Make your very best idea #1. That's the idea you should try first when you see someone being mean to another kid!

Something I Like to Do With Other People
A Sharing Circle

Objectives:

The students will:
— develop an understanding of group dynamics
— discuss what it takes to get along with others
— identify activities that bring them pleasure

Introducing the Topic:

In your own words, say to the students: *Today's topic is, "Something I Like to Do With Other People." It's fun to do things with other people. Most games require two or more people, as do many sports, such as football, baseball, even tennis. Think of something you like to do with other people. It might be shopping or talking on the phone. Perhaps you like big family picnics or holiday dinners. Or maybe you enjoy having lunch with friends. Do you have more fun at amusement parks when you are with a group? Think of one thing you like to do with other people and tell us about it. The topic is, "Something I Like to Do With Other People."*

Discussion questions:

1. What do we gain by experiencing events and activities with other people?
2. What happens when a group gets too large for a particular activity? What are the effects of having too few people?
3. What are some things you do when you're with others to show you're a good group member?

Social Awareness

Something I Did That Helped Someone Feel Good
A Sharing Circle

Objectives: The students will:
— identify feelings that are associated with positive acts.
— use their feelings to make positive decisions.
— develop empathy by examining times when they directly had an impact on someone else's good feelings.

Introduce the Topic: In your own words, say to the students: *Our topic today is, "Something I Did That Helped Someone Feel Good." We are all affected in some way by the behavior of others toward us. And we have the ability to influence how others feel. Think of a time when you deliberately did something that you knew would trigger a positive reaction in someone. Perhaps your friend was having a bad day and you said something funny that made them laugh. Perhaps you did an extra chore at home to help a family member who was feeling overworked. Think of the many things you have done because you wanted someone else to feel good, and share one example with us. Our topic is, "Something I Did That Helped Someone Feel Good."*

Discussion Questions:
1. How do you feel when you do something nice for someone else?
2. How do you benefit by doing something helpful for another person?
3. When we feel good about ourselves and when we help others, how are we affecting the world we live in?

A Way I Show Respect for Others
A Sharing Circle

Objective: The students will describe specific behaviors that demonstrate respect for others.

Introduce the Topic: In your own words, say to the students: *The topic for this discussion is, "A Way I Show Respect for Others." There are many ways that we can show respect for other people. Tell us about a way that you frequently use. Maybe you remember to say please and thank you, or try never to interrupt others when they're talking, or hold doors when you go through them so they won't swing back and smack the people behind you. Perhaps you try not to say critical things about others, or maybe you listen respectfully to the opinions of people you disagree with. Tell us what you do that is respectful, and how you learned to do it. Think about it for a few moments. The topic is, "A Way I Show Respect for Others".*

Discussion Questions:
1. How do you feel about yourself when you show respect for others?
2. If you want to be respected, will showing respect for others help? How?
3. Should we show respect for people we don't like? Explain.

Someone Did Something for Me That I Really Appreciated
A Sharing Circle

Objectives: The students will:
— explore positive feelings they experienced as a result of someone's kindness
— understand how thoughtful deeds benefit both giver and receiver

Introduce the Topic: In your own words, say to the students: *The topic of this session is, "Someone Did Something for Me That I Really Appreciated." You've probably all been on the receiving end of many thoughtful gestures. Think back over some of those experiences and choose one to share with us. Maybe a friend offered to give you a ride when you needed one, or helped you finish a report that you were struggling with. Perhaps a visiting relative presented you with a special treat, like your favorite cookie, candy, or snack. Or maybe someone listened when you needed to talk about a problem. Think for a moment about something like this that has happened to you. If you told the person how you felt, share that with us, too. The topic for today is, "Someone Did Something for Me That I Really Appreciated".*

Discussion Questions:
1. Did you notice any similarities in the kinds of things we appreciated?
2. How are people able to influence each other's feelings?
3. Wisdom says that one way to cheer yourself up when you're feeling low is to do something for someone else. What do you think of that idea?

Someone in Authority Whom I Respect
A Sharing Circle

Objectives: The students will:
—explore the dynamics of positive authority
—identify characteristics that command respect.

Introduce the Topic: In your own words, say to the students: *Our topic today is "Someone in Authority Whom I Respect." Does anyone come to mind who is in some kind of authority or leadership position and for whom you have a lot of respect? It may be someone who you know personally who is in some kind of a responsible position. It could be a teacher, parent, or a student who handles their leadership position well. Perhaps the person who comes to your mind is someone who holds public office or is a world leader of some kind. Can any of you think of someone like this? Take a minute to think about it. The topic is "Someone in Authority Whom I Respect."*

Discussion Questions:
1. Does "respect" mean the same as "like" to you? Explain.
2. If you were in an authority position, how would you gain respect?
3. Why is it important for someone in authority to earn the respect of others?
4. What are some things that can lead to a loss of respect?

My Reality Was Different from Someone Else's
A Sharing Circle

Objectives:

The students will:
— recognize that people can have different interpretations of the same situation.
— develop foundation skills for understanding others and appreciation of differences as well as similarities.

Introduce the Topic:

In your own words, say to the students: *Our topic today is "My Reality Was Different from Someone Else's." Native American's are famous for having their council meetings in a large circle. There are many important reasons for this. One of these reasons is that when something is placed in the middle of the circle, each person sees it a little differently. To the Native Americans this means that every person's perspective (view of reality) is different to some degree. Sometimes when we see or think about something in one way, we are surprised to find that someone else regards the same thing in a totally different way. Often we are both convinced that our reality is the correct one. This may affect our ability to make or keep friends, or make decisions. Think about it and see if you can find a time in your life when you've experienced this kind of situation. The topic is "My Reality Was Different from Someone Else's".*

Discussion Questions:

1. What really is real, and who decides the answer?
2. What can you learn about another person if you stop to consider their point of view?

Relationship Skills

Common To All
Experience Sheet and Discussion

Objectives: The students will:
—identify areas of interest.
—discuss how interests can be the basis for friendships and connection to others.

Materials: one copy of the Experience Sheet, "Things I Enjoy Doing" for each group of four students

Procedure: Begin the activity by asking the students to be thinking about the things they like to do in their free time. Break the students into groups of four. Pass out one Experience Sheet to each group. Ask the group members to each write their name on one of the numbered lines on their group sheet. Have each group select a recorder, or you may choose to assign the recorder job to one of the numbers on the sheet.

After allowing a few moments to think about things they like to do for enjoyment, have each group member, in numerical order, relate three or four favorite activities to their recorder who jots down the activities in the appropriate quadrant. After the four quadrants have been completed, have the students identify the enjoyable activities that are common to all. The recorder writes this list in the middle portion of the sheet. Ask a representative from each group (or call one of the numbers) to report to the entire class what enjoyable activities are held in common by their whole group.

Culminate the activity by asking these and other questions that help the students reflect on the value of mutual interests being the basis of friendships and healthy relationships.

Discussion Questions:

1. What are some of the feelings we get when we are engaged in a favorite pastime?
2. Did you learn of someone's interest in something that you didn't know before?
3. Were there any interesting similarities in interests?
4. Were there any interesting differences in interests?
5. Discuss how mutual interests can form the basis of a relationship.
6. How can you build on things you hold in common with someone else to develop a new friendship or strengthen an existing friendship?
7. Did you hear about something new that you would like to know more about?

Things I Enjoy Doing
Experience Sheet

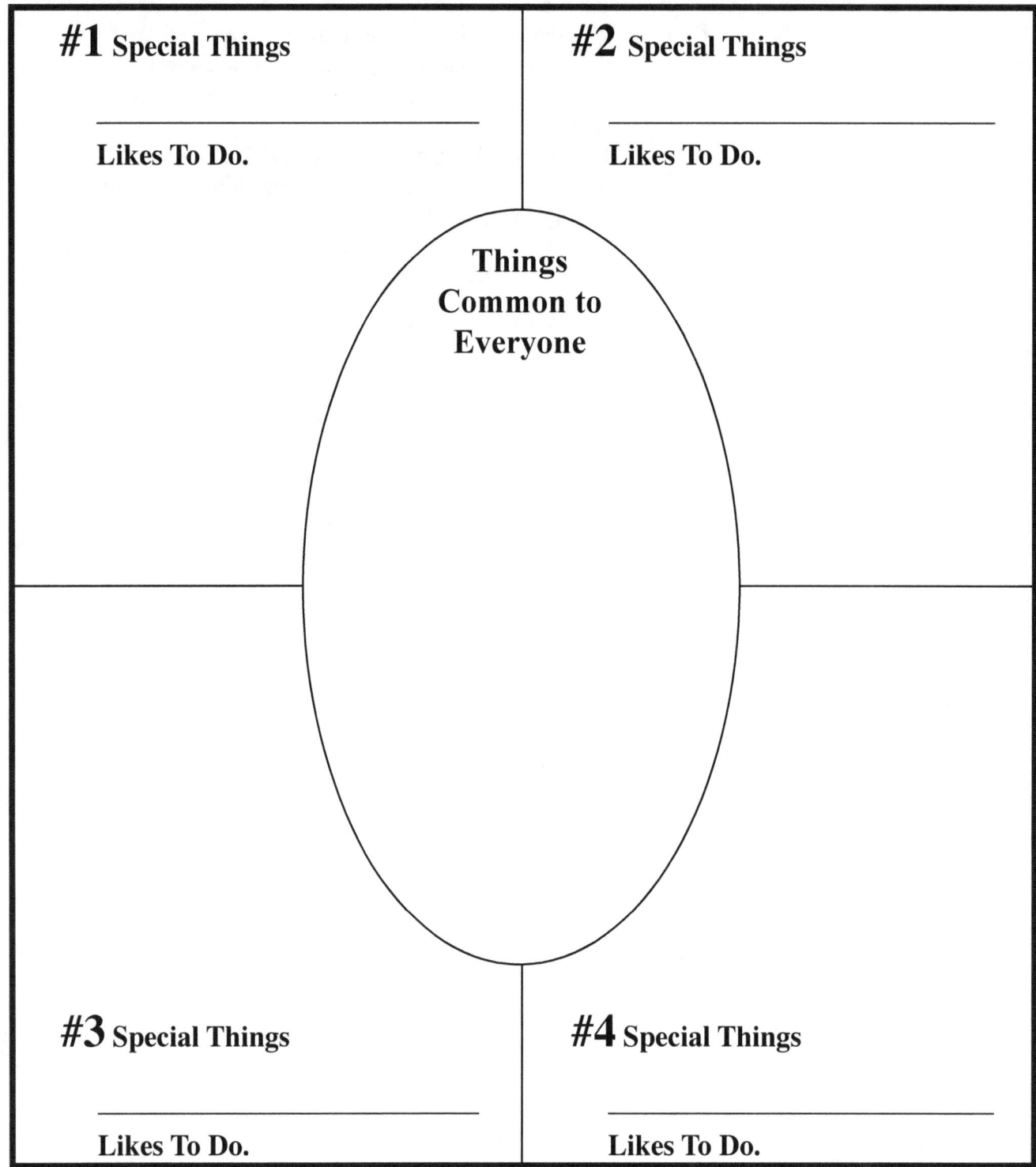

How to be an Active Listener
Communication Skill Practice

Objectives: The students will:
—define the role of the listener in communication.
—identify and demonstrate "active listening" behaviors.

Materials: a diagrammatic model of the communications process (see below) drawn on the board; a list of topics written on the board (see end of activity); one copy of the experience sheet, "Be an Active Listener!" for each student

Procedure: On the board, draw a simple diagram illustrating the communication process. For example, print the words, SPEAKER and LISTENER and draw two arrows — one going in each direction — between the two words.

SPEAKER ⇌ LISTENER

Explain to the students that in order for two people to enjoy and encourage each other, to work, play, or solve problems together, they need to be able to communicate effectively. In your own words, say: *In every example of communication, no matter how small, a message is sent from one person (the speaker) to the other person (the listener). The message is supposed to tell the listener something about the feelings and/or thoughts of the speaker. Because the speaker cannot "give" the listener his or her feelings and thoughts, they have to be "coded" in words. Good communicators pick words that describe their feelings and thoughts as closely as possible. Nonverbal "signals" almost always accompany the verbal message; for example, a smile, a frown, or a hand gesture. Sometimes the entire message is nonverbal. Good communicators send nonverbal signals that exactly match their feelings and thoughts.*

Ask the students to describe what a good listener says and does to show that they are interested in what the speaker is saying and is really listening. Write their ideas on the board. Be sure to include these behaviors:

1. Face the speaker.
2. Look into the speaker's eyes but without staring.
3. Be relaxed, but attentive.

4. Listen to the words and try to picture in your own mind what the speaker is saying.
5. Don't interrupt or fidget. When it is your turn to respond, don't change the subject or start telling your own story.
6. If you don't understand something, wait for the speaker to pause and then ask, "What do you mean by..."
7. Try to feel what the speaker is feeling (show empathy).
8. Respond in ways that let the speaker know that you are listening and understand what is being said. Ways of responding might include nodding, saying "uh huh," or giving feedback that proves you are listening, for example:

- **Briefly summarize:** "You're saying that you might have to quit the team in order to have time for a paper route."
- **Restate feelings, showing empathy:** "You must be feeling pretty bad." or "You sound really happy!"

Tell the students that this type of listening is called active listening. Ask them if they can explain why the word active is used to describe it.

Move on to the next part of the activity by asking the students to form groups of three. Tell them to decide who is A, who is B, and who is C. Announce that you are going to give the students an opportunity to practice active listening. Explain the process:

In the first round, A will be the speaker and B will be the listener and will use active listening. C will be the observer. C's job is to notice how well B listens, and report their observations at the end of the round. I will be the timekeeper. We will have three rounds, so that you can each have a turn in all three roles. When you are the speaker, pick a topic from the list on the board, and remember to pause occasionally so that the listener can respond with active listening.

Signal the start of the first round. Call time after two minutes. Have the observers give feedback for one minute. Tell the students to switch roles. Conduct two more rounds.

Lead a follow-up discussion. Using these and your own questions to help the students reflect on what makes a good listener.

Discussion Questions:
1. How did it feel to "active listen?"
2. How difficult was it to feel empathy for your partner?
3. What was it like to be the observer?
4. When you were the speaker, how did you feel having someone really empathize with and listen to you?
5. What was easiest about active listening? What was hardest?
6. What did you learn from your observer?
7. Why is it important to learn to be a good listener?

Conclude the activity by passing out the Experience Sheet. Provide time for the students to complete it and with their original groups of three have them share the three things they identified they could do to become better listeners.

List of topics:
"A Time I Needed Some Help"
"Something I'd Like to Do Better"
"A Problem I Need to Solve"
"The Best Gift I Ever Received"
"A Time I Got Into an Argument"
"I Feel Happiest When…"
"A Tough Decision I Had to Make"
"Something I'd Like to Be or Do When I'm an Adult"
"My Favorite Family Tradition"

Be an Active Listener!
Experience Sheet

Listening is a very important part of good communication. Listed below are characteristics of a good listener. Check the ones that describe you most of the time.

A good listener:

___ Faces the speaker.

___ Looks into the speaker's eyes without staring.

___ Is relaxed, but attentive.

___ keeps an open mind.

___ Listens to the words and tries to picture what the speaker is saying.

___ Doesn't interrupt or fidget.

___ Waits for the speaker to pause before asking clarifying questions.

___ Tries to feel what the speaker is feeling (feels and shows empathy).

___ Nods and says "uh huh," or summarizes to let the speaker know they're listening.

Listening is a skill that can be learned and improved upon, but it requires both your *attention* and your *intention* to really listen. Honest listening requires that you make sense of the speaker's words and pay attention to their tone of voice, and body language. But, the hardest thing of all is to be able to block out distractions and thoughts of what you will be saying. Keeping your attention on the speaker is the essence of good listening.

What does this proverb mean to you?
   "We have two ears and one mouth so we can listen twice as much as we speak."

_____

_____

What are your two strongest qualities as a listener?

1. _____

2. _____

What is your weakest quality as a listener?

_____

What are three things you can do to become a better listener?

1. _____

2. _____

3. _____

Dear Mable . . .
Creative Writing and Discussion

Objectives: The students will:
— write about a real problem.
— attempt to empathize with and describe possible solutions to someone else's problem.

Materials: paper, a collection box (for problems), and bulletin boards for posting letters and responses

Procedure: Read aloud a newspaper or on-line advice column to which readers write with problems and in which the columnist offers advice and solutions.

Ask the students to write a brief letter to "Mable." Assure them that Mable will respond. Explain that the letter should consist of a request for advice concerning a real problem, present or past. Urge the students to include enough facts and clues as to the emotions of the people involved to allow someone reading the letter to empathize with their feelings and point of view. If the students can't think of a problem of their own to describe, tell them its okay to describe someone else's problem, as long as they know enough about it to be specific. Ask the students to sign their letters with fictitious names, and drop them into the collection box.

Have each student reach into the box and draw out a letter. Instruct the students to prepare an answer to the letter. Allow the students to consult with each other in small groups to generate ideas for thoughtful, empathic responses. The rest of the period can be devoted to writing. Ask the students to sign their real names to their response.

Collect and read the letters and responses. Correct the responses only, and offer the students an opportunity to rewrite them. Have the students post their letters and responses on a class bulletin board. Give the students time to circulate and read each other's letters and responses.

Conclude the activity by asking these and your own questions to help students reflect on their learning.

Discussion Questions:
1. What was hardest about this assignment? What was easiest?
2. How much empathy did you, as "Mable," feel for your correspondent in the situation they described?
3. What kinds of questions did you, as "Mable," want to ask your correspondent?
4. How did lack of personal contact affect your ability to empathize with the situation?

Cooperative vs. Competitive
Stories and Discussion

Objectives: The students will:
—distinguish between cooperative and competitive behaviors.
—describe the benefits and drawbacks of cooperative and competitive behaviors.
—identify ways that the class can be more cooperative.

Materials: whiteboard

Procedure: Read the following story to the students.

Mr. Monday's class was getting ready for the science fair. The students worked on their projects every day, independently and quietly. First they researched different project ideas. Then they met individually with Mr. Monday to decide what to work on. If a student couldn't come up with an idea, Mr. Monday assigned one. When the students had a question or got stumped, Mr. Monday often sent them to the library to find answers in reference books. Mr. Monday urged the students to keep their projects under wraps and their findings secret, so that everyone would be surprised on the opening day of the fair. The students assembled their displays at home and didn't bring them to school until the day before the fair. Mr. Monday reminded the students that the judges would be awarding prizes for the best entries.

Ms. Friday's class was getting ready for the science fair, too. First, small groups of students researched possible project topics. Then the groups compiled their ideas in one big list and the entire class chose eight projects to work on. The students formed eight teams. Students who weren't sure which team they wanted to belong to were allowed to work on more than one team until they decided. Ms. Friday encouraged all the teams to share ideas with one another. About once a week, she called an "Investigator's Forum" where each team reported on the status of its project, and where everyone offered suggestions and brainstormed ideas to make the projects better. The groups built their displays in class, sometimes staying after school to put in extra time. There was a lot of moving around Ms. Friday's class, and quite a bit of noise, too. Ms. Friday told the students that she wanted all the projects to be the best they could be.

Write the headings "Competitive" and Cooperative" on the board. Ask the students which label fits Mr. Monday's class and which fits Ms. Friday's class. Then ask them to recall specific attitudes and behaviors in each story that were competitive and cooperative. Write their ideas on the board under the appropriate heading. For example:

Mr. Monday/Competitive
    worked alone
    kept projects secret
    didn't share ideas
    concentrated on winning prizes

Ms. Friday/Cooperative
    worked in teams
    shared ideas
    did joint problem solving
    talked freely
    concentrated to making all projects excellent

Conclude the activity with a total class discussion.

Discussion Questions:

1. What are the benefits of cooperating with others? What are the drawbacks?
2. What are the benefits of competing with others? What are the drawbacks?
3. What cooperative projects have you been a part of? Tell us what the experience was like for you.

How Do Things Stack Up?
A Cooperative Team Experience

Objectives: The students will:
—work cooperatively to build structures out of books.
—identify specific cooperative and competitive behaviors and describe how they affect completion of a team task.

Materials: lots of hard covered books (Instead of books, alternative building materials could be marshmallows and spaghetti or gum drops and tooth picks.).

Procedure: Ask the students to form teams of five to eight. Have each team sit around a table, and select one member to be its Observer. Announce that all other team members are players. Provide each team with easy access to the books.

Explain that each team will work cooperatively to build a structure out of books. This "house of books" can have many angles and be multi-tiered. Encourage the teams to be imaginative and create their own "architectural masterpiece".

Take the Observers aside and say to them: Your job is to stand beside the table while your team is putting together the book structure and to notice what happens. Be prepared to describe such things as how well the group works together, who shares books and ideas and who does not; who makes an effort to include everyone and who does not; whether members concentrate only on the structure in front of them or watch the progress of all the teams; cooperative vs. competitive behaviors; any conflicts that occur and how they are resolved; who provides leadership.

Read aloud the following rules of play:
- Your task as a team is to assemble the largest book structure you can.
- Time will be called at the end of 15 minutes.
- Teams are encouraged to use books of all sizes and as many books as you need.
- Members of each team must work cooperatively, contributing books and suggestions to the building of the structure.
- If the structure collapses, you may start over and continue working until time is called

Give the signal to start play. Roam around the room observing the teams in action. You may want to make some comments based on what you observed during the time allotted for feedback from the observers. Your observations may also give you ideas for additional discussion questions.

At the conclusion of play give each team a few moments of "fame" as they display their structure to the other teams. Next, have the Observers give feedback to their team on what they observed. If several teams are playing, have the Observers do this simultaneously. Advise the teams to listen carefully, and not to interrupt, argue with, or put down the Observer.

Conclude the activity by leading a whole class discussion helping the students to reflect on the benefits of cooperative behavior.

Discussion Questions:

1. What did you learn from your Observer?
2. What was the object of the game?
3. Which kind of behavior was most effective in this activity, cooperative or competitive? Why?
4. What are some of the effects of competitive behavior on a team? ... of cooperative behavior?
5. If anyone emerged as a leader in your group, how did that person demonstrate his or her leadership.
6. If you could play the game again, would you change your own behavior?
7. What did you learn from this experience?

Relationship Skills

What's Your Preference — Alone or Together?
Team Experiment and Discussion

Objectives: The students will:
—demonstrate the power of team efforts.
—describe advantages of working with a team. ...of working alone.
—identify their preferred way of working — alone or with a group.

Materials: a watch/clock with a second hand; whiteboard; writing materials for each student

Procedure: Have the students form teams of four or five. From the following list, select one word for each team. Write the assigned words on the board so all of the groups can see their word.

    identification
    reverberation
    heterogeneous
    responsiveness
    haberdasher
    refrigeration
    significantly
    predetermination
    simultaneous

Explain to the students that, working individually, they are to write as many words as they can, using the letters in the word that has been assigned to them. Go over the rules, saying: *There will be NO talking. You must write real words of two or more letters using only the letters in the assigned word. For example, if your assigned word contains only one "a," then new words you come up with must contain no more than one "a." However, you may use the "a" in more than one word. You will have 5 minutes to come up with as many words as possible.*

Call time at the end of 5 minutes. Explain to the students that in the second round of the activity, they are to follow the same rules, however, this time they will be working together as a team, and they can talk with their teammates. Assign each team a new word from the list. Again, allow 5 minutes for each team to brainstorm as many words as it can..

Poll the teams to find out how many words they came up with while working alone and how many they came up with working as a team. (Chances are the team efforts produced more words.) Hold a culminating discussion. Encourage the students to hypothesize as to why they obtained the results they reported.

Discussion Questions:
1. How did you feel when you were working alone?
2. How did you feel when you were part of a team?
3. Under which circumstances — alone or with a team — did you produce more words? Under which circumstances did you enjoy yourself more?
4. Why do team efforts often produce better results than individual efforts?
5. If you prefer working with a team, what are some things you can do to make yourself more effective when you work alone?
6. If you like to work alone, what are some things you can do to be more effective when you are part of a team?

The Spirit Club
A Group Decision-Making Game

Objectives: The students will:
—work as a group to reach a decision.
—describe how roles played by individuals affect group dynamics and task completion.
—identify individual "agendas" and describe how they affect the group.

Materials: one set of nine 3-inch by 5-inch Role Cards, each card printed with a role description (see below)

Procedure: In advance, print the following role descriptions on the nine cards:

1. **Information Giver:** You point out facts, ask questions, and give information.
2. **Evaluator:** You encourage the group to talk about the pros and cons of each suggestion. You secretly decide that you will support the idea that is best supported by facts and information.
3. **Clarifier:** You try to make sure everyone understands every idea and suggestion.
4. **Topic Switcher:** You keep getting off the subject.
5. **Facilitator:** You help others participate and suggest ways to share ideas.
6. **Harmonizer:** You try to ease tension and settle any conflicts that occur.
7. **Leader:** You want to be the leader of the group. To become the leader, you attempt to take charge of the meeting.
8. **Clown:** You get bored, and start telling jokes to try to make the task more fun. You secretly hope the money will be used toward a trip to Disney World.
9. **Dropout:** You think the faculty advisor and school administrators should make the decision. You say so, and then back off.

Choose from ten to fifteen volunteers to participate in the decision-making game. Have them move their desks or chairs into a circle near the center of the room. Have the remaining students form an outer circle, and announce that they will be observers. Instruct the observers to take notes so that they can describe what they see to the class in a follow-up discussion. Suggest that they pay attention to both content (what happens) and process (how it happens).

Read the task to the players: *You belong to the Spirit Club here at school. The club sponsors dances and other special events. The club pays for the events it sponsors by selling soft drinks, hot dogs, and snacks at games, concerts, and other school functions. This year, the club has made a lot more money than expected. After all expenses and special events have been paid for, there is still $5,000 left. Your task, as a member of the club, is to decide how the extra money should be used. The club's faculty advisor has said that she will support any responsible decision the club makes.*

Randomly distribute the role cards to the players. Tell them to memorize their role and then put the card away or give it back to you. Caution them NOT to divulge their role to other players. If any players have questions about their roles, assist them privately. Instruct those without role cards to play themselves.

Convene the meeting, playing the part of the faculty advisor. Answer any questions the committee members have about the task, and then announce that you have an errand to run and will return in 20 minutes. Take your place among the observers.

At the end of 20 minutes, stop the meeting and lead a debriefing session. Use these and other open-ended questions to debrief the players. Then ask the observers to describe their observations. During any remaining time, facilitate a total class discussion.

Discussion Questions:
1. How did you feel in your role?
2. What problems did you have playing your role?
3. What behaviors were most helpful to the group?
4. What behaviors were least helpful?
5. What would have helped the group reach a decision more easily?
6. How did the "hidden agendas" of some group members affect the process?
7. How was this like real group situations you've experienced?
8. What did you learn from this activity?

Variation: Design a situation more in keeping with the interests and experiences of your students. The role definitions and discussion questions are generic; only the hidden agenda of the "clown" will need to be modified.

Put-downs Aren't Cool
Survey and Discussion

Objectives: The students will:
—identify negative consequences of put down behaviors.
—identify some of the reasons that people put others down.
—empathize with the receiver of put-down statements.

Materials: paper and pencils

Procedure: Tell the students that today you want to focus on a way of talking that is very common at school. Explain that talking this way often starts out as a form of joking around or teasing, and then turns into a habit that continues without thought. Unfortunately, this habit can be hurtful to others and serves no real purpose. Ask the students to guess what you're talking about. Give them a few moments and if no one guesses *put-downs or putting others down*, write the term on the board.

Ask the students to help you make a list of all the statements they remember hearing people say that put others down. As the students give you the words, write them on the board, enclosing each phrase in quotation marks, *e.g.*, "You'd forget your head if it weren't attached."

Talk about the nature of put-downs. Ask the students:
—*Why do people put each other down?*
—*When a put-down has been directed at you, how did it make you feel?*
—*Are some put-downs worse than others? Which ones?*
—*How can a person tell the difference between a put-down that is meant as a joke and a put-down that is meant as verbal abuse (is intentionally hurtful)?*

Give the students the following assignment: *For the next 24 hours, I want you to carry a pencil and a piece of paper with you and write down every put-down statement that you hear. Write down put-downs that are directed at you, and put-downs that you overhear between others. Record put-downs you hear on any TV shows or through social media, too. Bring your list to class tomorrow* (or designate another day).

When the students return have them take out their put-down surveys. While you record examples on the board, go around the room and have each student read several items from his or her list.

When everyone has had a turn to contribute, ask if there are any additional put-downs that should be added to the list especially any they have heard at school. Then, go back and categorize and tally the examples. Here are three possible categories.
1. Reflex put-downs (result of an unconscious communication habit)
2. Teasing or joking put-downs
3. Malicious (intentionally hurtful) put-downs

Discuss the different motivations that lead to each type of put-down, emphasizing that *all* types have a negative impact and are often interpreted by the receiver as intentionally hurtful. Complete the activity by breaking the students into groups of 4 or 5. Have the groups brainstorm ideas for ending put downs among themselves and in the school. Allow time for brainstorming and then have each group present its list of ideas for ending put downs. Use the questions below to stimulate further discussion, or formulate questions of your own.

Discussion Questions:

1. Why do put-downs hurt feelings?
2. How can you respond to people who tease you? ...bully you? ....insult you?
3. How can you break the habit of putting others down?
4. How can we help each other to remember not to use put downs?
5. What would our school be like if no one used put downs?

Friends
Class Discussion and Experience Sheet

Objectives: The students will:
—describe positive and negative qualities of friendships
—discuss how to make and keep friends.

Materials: one copy of the experience sheet "What Is a Real Friend?" for each student; whiteboard

Procedure: On the board write the word **"friendships,"** and underneath write the headings, **"positive"** and **"negative"** next to each other.

Lead an introductory discussion on the subject of friendship. Begin by emphasizing that there are both positive and negative friendships. Elaborate on the notion that positive friendships are based on the healthy, positive qualities that each person contributes to the relationship, and negative friendships are based on unhealthy, negative qualities and frequently lead to stressful relationships.

Ask the students to name and discuss positive reasons for choosing a friend. List their reasons under the appropriate heading. (You may want to provide the first one or two examples.) Then list and discuss several examples of negative reasons, including some of your own.

At the conclusion of the discussion, distribute the experience sheet, "What Is A Real Friend?" Review the prodedure and have the students fill it out. Allow the students to talk among themselves as they work.

When the students have completed their experience sheets, ask these and other relevant questions to help them reflect on their learnings.

Discussion Questions:
1. Why do you think people stay in negative friendships?
2. Why do you think it's important to have positive friendships?
3. What kinds of things happen in negative friendships?
4. What kinds of things happen in positive friendships?

What Is a Real Friend?
Experience Sheet

	YES	NO
1. A friend is someone who knows all about me and likes me at the same time.		
2. A friend is someone who always agrees with me.		
3. A friend is someone who doesn't care how expensive my clothes are.		
4. A friend is someone who'll do whatever I say.		
5. A friend is someone who listens to me even if I am talking about my troubles.		
6. A friend is someone who expects me to see things exactly the way they do.		

If you said yes to numbers 1, 3, and 5, you have probably had some real friends. They knew and like you just the way you are. They also cared how you felt. They listened to your feelings. That's how they proved they were friends.

If you answered no to numbers 2, 4, and 6, you realize that everybody's different and that's okay. Friends don't have to agree with each other all of the time. And they don't always have to do what each other wants, to prove their friendship.

Think of a friend you had when you were a child:
What did you like about him or her? _____

_____

What do you think he or she liked about you? _____

_____

What was one of the best times you ever had together? _____

_____

Think about someone who is a friend of yours now:
How did your friendship begin? _____
_____

What are some things you like to do together? _____
_____

What is different about your friendship now from the way it was in
the beginning? _____
_____

Have you ever had a friendship that didn't seem good for you? What was it about the friendship that wasn't good? _____
_____

What do you think you would do if you wanted to be friends with someone who spoke a different language?	How do you think you'd make friends with someone who has a vision problem? Or is hearing impaired?
What do you think you'd do if a friend of yours started doing something you thought was dangerous?	

List the most important things you want in a friend.

1. _____   4. _____

2. _____   5. _____

3. _____   6. _____

Getting to Know You
Experience Sheet and Discussion

Objectives: The students will:
—describe how a friendship developed.
—identify ways they meet people and make friends.
—state the benefits of enlarging one's repertoire of social skills.

Materials: one copy of the experience sheet, "Getting to Know You" for each student

Procedure: Ask the students to think of a friend they currently have, or one they used to have. Invite volunteers to tell the group how they met this person and how the friendship developed. Compare and contrast the various ways in which people can meet.

Distribute the experience sheets and briefly review the directions. Give the students time to complete the sheet.

If the group is large, have the students share their completed experience sheets in smaller groupings (three to five). If the group is small, complete this portion of the activity as a total group. Have the student's share the techniques they would like to learn better and brainstorm with each other how they might do that.

Lead a culminating discussion. Focus on the benefits of being comfortable with and using many different approaches.

Discussion Questions:
1. Which techniques for making friends are you most comfortable with?
2. Which ways of making friends would you like to become better at?
3. Which ways are you least comfortable with when another person uses them with you?
4. Why is it easy for some people to make friends and harder for others?

Getting to Know You
Experience Sheet

Below are some things that people do to meet and get to know others. Read each item. Check "YES" if it is something you do often. Check "NO" if it is something you almost never do. Check "SOMETIMES" if it is something you do occasionally.

1. **Introduce yourself.** This is a great skill to have. Most people are hesitant to walk up to someone they don't know and introduce themselves. So take the lead.

    ____YES ____ NO ____SOMETIMES

2. **Smile.** Sincere smiles are warm and welcoming. They show that you are friendly, and they make other people feel good.

    ____YES ____ NO ____SOMETIMES

3. **Start a conversation.** One of the best ways to start a conversation is to say something about yourself and then ask a question. For example: "I can hardly wait for Spring vacation. My family is going camping. What are you going to do?"

    ____YES ____ NO ____SOMETIMES

4. **Compliment people.** Be generous with praise. When you really like someone's clothes, haircut, drawing or report, say so. Tell a person when you think he or she played a sport or game well.

    ____YES ____ NO ____SOMETIMES

5. **Join organizations; take part in activities.** By joining a club or participating in an activity, you meet people who have interests similar to yours. It's one of the best ways to make friends.

    ____YES ____ NO ____SOMETIMES

6. **Say thank you.** Everyone likes to be appreciated. When someone helps you out, even a little, be sure to show your appreciation.

   ____YES ____ NO ____SOMETIMES

7. **Run for office.** Good leaders are always in demand. Being a leader puts you in the thick of things where you are sure to get to know people.

   ____YES ____ NO ____SOMETIMES

8. **Be a good listener.** Listening to someone shows that you care. Become a good listener and people will seek you out. Why? Because we all like to be listened to, and good listeners are hard to find.

   ____YES ____ NO ____SOMETIMES

9. **Offer to help.** Carry a book, loan a pencil, help solve a problem — notice when people are struggling and offer your assistance. However, always ask first. Sometimes people don't want help.

   ____YES ____ NO ____SOMETIMES

10. **Remember names and use them.** Names are important to people. Using them shows caring and respect.

    ____YES ____ NO ____SOMETIMES

11. **Give parties.** A party doesn't have to be fancy. Just invite some interesting people to get together. Include people you don't know well.

    ____YES ____ NO ____SOMETIMES

12. **Make people laugh.** Laughing feels good. If you can share a funny joke or story once in awhile, people will enjoy being around you. Try not to be a constant clown.

    ____YES ____ NO ____SOMETIMES

Go back and circle one or two techniques you'd like to learn or use better.

Strength In Diversity
Brainstorm and Discussion

Objectives: The students will;
— name specific ways in which people are different and the same.
— demonstrate that individual perception determines whether a characteristic is seen as a difference or a commonality.
— recognize commonalities as vital to achieving understanding and harmony.

Materials: whiteboard

Procedure: Draw a horizontal line on the board, dividing a section of the board approximately in half. At the top of the board, write the heading, "Different." Begin the activity by asking the students to name all of the ways that human beings differ from one another. Write their suggestions below the heading and above the line. You will probably list such items as personality, preferences, skills, intelligence, traditions, culture, race, gender, abilities, physical appearance, socioeconomic status, etc. Keep going until the space above the line is crowded with items.

Write the heading, "Same," just below the horizontal line. Ask the students to name all of the ways in which humans are exactly the same. Suggestions will come more slowly this time. Be patient and see if someone comes up with the idea that all the items written above the line also represent ways in which people are exactly alike. (The idea is that all people possess personalities, skills, intelligence, etc., even though these attributes differ qualitatively from one person to another. In fact, this can be said for every item written above the line. All of these things not only make people different, they also make them the same.) If one of the students makes this observation, proceed from there. If no one discovers the concept, explain that you can add greatly to the list, and begin underlining items above the line, saying something like, *We all have different personalities, but we all have a personality*, etc. Make the point that people are as much alike as they are different.

Explain that whether we see these items as differences or commonalities depends on our perception. When we focus only on the ways we differ, we tend to grow apart, but when we focus on commonalities, we tend to come together. This coming together creates strength in diversity. It can be thought of, too, as unity through diversity or common ground.

Tell the students that ALL successful teams are built on diversity. Using the example of personalities, demonstrate how everyone on a team has an individual personality, and that together those personalities make up the team personality. Members have different talents, skills, and knowledge to bring to a team. These differences are what make teams strong. Without diversity, a team cannot have much strength.

When individuals believe that their differences make them right or better (and make others wrong or worse) conflicts occur and prejudices develop. The need to see our differences as "right" or "wrong" destroys our ability to work together effectively. Encourage discussion by asking these and other questions.

Discussion Questions:

1. What are some ways in which all people benefit from individual differences?
2. How can differences among group members contribute to their efforts when working on a joint endeavor?
3. How does the need to be "right" interfere with efforts to build on diversity?
4. Why do you think the world needs differences?
5. Why do we sometimes see differences as positive and at other times as negative?
6. How can we emphasize the positive aspects of diversity?

How It Feels To Be Left Out
Creative Writing and Discussion

Objectives: The students will;
— identify how it feels to be rejected or excluded.
— acknowledge their feelings about those who are different from them.
— develop empathy by identifying with the difficulties of others.

Materials: writing materials

Procedure: Explain to the students that you would like them to write about the topic, "How It Feels to Be Left Out." Emphasize that they will need to use their imaginations, because they are going to write from the viewpoint of a person of a different race or culture, or a person with a disability.

In your own words, explain to the students: *Imagine a situation in which a person might be excluded. Think about how you feel when you are left out of a group or activity in which you really want to participate. How might the situation and/or the feelings, be the same or different for someone of a different race or culture, or someone with a disability? If the feelings would be about the same, what would they be? If the feelings would be different, how would they be different, and what would they be like? You might begin your story when the person is just starting to think about joining the group or activity. Describe what happens that leads to the rejection, and concentrate on the expression of feelings throughout.*

Ask the students to indicate at the end of their papers whether or not they would be willing to read their story to the class. Collect the papers and evaluate them in your usual manner, then return them to the students. Ask volunteers to read their stories to the class. Facilitate a discussion after each reading, basing your questions on issues presented in the story. Conclude the activity with a general discussion.

Discussion Questions:

1. How are the feelings of most people the same in response to rejection? How are they different for people who belong to a minority race or culture? ... for people who have a disability?
2. What did you discover about your own attitudes towards people who belong to minorities or have disabilities?
3. What good does it do to try to understand each other's feelings?
4. What new ideas did you get about rejecting others? ... about handling rejection? ... about the idea of inclusion?

The Clique Phenomenon
Experience Sheet and Discussion

Objectives: The students will:
—identify ways to make new friends.
—state the effects of cliques on those left out.
—develop and follow through on a plan to make at least one new friend.

Materials: whiteboard; one copy of the experience sheet, "Getting On Your Own Side," for each student

Procedure: Have the students form two teams. Give the teams 10 to 15 minutes to brainstorm a list describing as many ways as they can think of to make new friends. At the end of the allotted time, reconvene the class and ask the groups to share their lists. Possible ideas include:
- Sit beside someone different in the cafeteria and say hello.
- Offer to show someone new around the school.
- Join a school organization.
- Offer to help someone carry a heavy load.
- Team up with someone you don't know very well to work on a class project.
- Run an ad in the school paper asking for a companion for particular activities, like hiking or bicycling.
- Ask someone you know to introduce you to new people.
- Go to the gym or track after school and say hello to the kids who are practicing.

Write the word clique on the board and ask the students to help you define it. One possible definition might be: An in-group or gang of kids that defines itself as much by who is excluded as by who is included.

Discuss how a clique's policy of exclusion causes members to have difficulty making new friends, and can completely frustrate the efforts of someone who is not in the clique to become good friends with someone who is. Stress that the reason many kids want to be a part of a clique is that they want to be liked by "important" people and feel important themselves. Also point out that generally cliques consist of people from the same cultural, ethnic or racial backgrounds. Cliques usually exclude anyone "different" from their members.

Pass out a copy of the experience sheet, "Getting On Your Own Side" to each student. Allow the students about 10 minutes to complete the sheet. Then ask them to rejoin their teams and (voluntarily) share their answers to the questions.

Encourage the students to commit to making one new friend in the next week or including one new person in their existing group of friends. Explain that this assignment carries one important restriction: The person they befriend or include in their group should be different from them (or the group) in some way.

Stipulate that before they can claim to have completed the assignment, the students must do something tangible with the new friend, such as sit together at an assembly, eat lunch together, go jogging or bicycling together, visit each other's home, see a movie together, or play video games after school. Ask the students to pay particular attention to the "clique phenomenon" and avoid doing anything that causes another person to feel left out. Set a time for the students to report back on their endeavor to make a new friend.

Conclude the initial activity with a discussion helping the students to reflect on the negative aspects of cliques and the benefits of inclusion.

Discussion Questions:
1. In what ways do you think cliques are good?
2. In what ways do you think cliques are harmful?
3. In what ways do the members of a clique miss out when they exclude others that are different from them?
4. Of what value to a group is having varied membership?
5. Have you ever wanted to belong to a clique? If so, why was it important?
6. What would happen if there were no cliques at this school?
7. What kinds of cliques do adults have?

Relationship Skills

Getting on Your Own Side
Experience Sheet

Is it worth it to be in?
What have you done to be included In a group?

I have...

__Yes __No	• risked losing friends.
__Yes __No	• hurt people who thought they were my friends by making them feel left out.
__Yes __No	• done something I thought was not right.
__Yes __No	• done something I knew was against the law.
__Yes __No	• drunk alcohol or used drugs.
__Yes __No	• done something that might have harmed me physically.
__Yes __No	• done something that cost me a lot of money.
__Yes __No	• done something that interfered with my school work.
__Yes __No	• done something my parents would have objected to if they had known.
__Yes __No	• done whatever was necessary, as long as it didn't harm anyone else.
__Yes __No	• done something that was against my religion.
__Yes __No	• done whatever was necessary.

Can you remember a time when you were pressured to exclude someone from an activity?

How did you feel?

What did you do?

If this ever happens again, what do you think you will do?

A Time I Put Myself in Someone Else's Shoes
A Sharing Circle

Objectives: The students will:
— describe instances of perspective-taking
— explain how perspective taking contributes to interpersonal understanding and problem solving.

Introduce the Topic: In your own words say: *Our topic for this session is, "A Time I Put Myself in Someone Else's Shoes." Do you know what that expression means? Putting yourself in someone else's shoes means seeing and feeling things from that person's point of view. Think of a time when you tried very hard to understand how someone was thinking or feeling by imagining what it would be like to be in that person's shoes. Maybe you had a conflict with a friend and tried to see the conflict the way they did. Or maybe you wanted to better understand how a situation looked to someone from a different culture, so you asked questions and listened carefully to that person's answers. Have you ever tried to understand what it would be like to be blind, or to have some other kind of disability? Have you ever tried to understand how someone feels who cannot speak your language? Taking the perspective of another person helps us to understand or* **empathize** *with that person. Tell us what you learned by walking in someone else's shoes. Our topic is, "A Time I Put Myself in Someone Else's Shoes."*

Discussion Questions:
1. How did it feel to put yourself in someone else's shoes?
2. What do you need to do in order to understand another person's point of view?
3. How does empathizing with others help us solve problems and resolve conflicts?
4. How do you feel when a person refuses to understand where you are coming from?
5. What would the world be like if people and countries were unwilling to understand each other's points of view?

I Didn't Say a Word, But They Knew How I Felt
A Sharing Circle

Objectives: The students will:
—recall a time when someone empathized with them by accurately reading nonverbal cues.
—recognize that feelings are conveyed primarily through nonverbal means.
—describe how it feels to gain someone's empathy and understanding.

Introduce the Topic: In your own words say: *Our topic for today is, "I Didn't Say a Word, But They Knew How I Felt." We've talked about empathy — about being able to determine the feelings of others without their telling us. In this circle, think of a time when another person, or a group of people, knew how you were feeling, even though you didn't tell them. Maybe you were disappointed, joyful, embarrassed, confused, angry, or thrilled. Whatever the feeling was, someone could see it in you, and told you so. Someone empathized with your feelings. Take a few minutes to think of such a time. The topic is, "I Didn't Say a Word, But They Knew How I Felt."*

Discussion Questions:
1. How do you think the others knew what you were feeling?
2. How did you feel when someone empathized with your feelings?
3. How do you feel when someone refuses to empathize, or even understand, your feelings though you've made them very clear?

What I Think Good Communication Is
A Sharing Circle

Objectives: The students will:
—describe elements of good communication.
—discuss feelings generated by good and bad communication.

Introduce the Topic: In your own words say: *Today's topic for discussion is, "What I Think Good Communication Is." Communication is an exchange of thoughts, feelings, opinions, or information between two or more people. Today we're going to focus on the ingredients of good communication. There are no right or wrong answers; whatever you contribute will help us develop a better understanding of what's involved. If you like, try thinking about a person with whom you've had particular success communicating and attempt to isolate some of the things that happen during your interactions with that person. Take a few minutes, and then we'll begin sharing on our topic, "What I Think Good Communication Is."*

Discussion Questions:
1. What quality or ingredient of good communication was mentioned most often during our sharing?
2. How do you feel after experiencing good communication? ...bad communication?
3. Why is it important to practice good communication?

A Time I Worked in a Successful Group
A Sharing Circle

Objectives: The students will:
—describe characteristics of a successful group.
—describe their contributions to the success of a group.
—state that a successful group needs the diverse abilities of all its members.

Introduce the Topic: In your own words say: *All of us have belonged to a group that has had some form of success. Successful groups have certain characteristics in common. One of these characteristics is interdependence. Interdependence exists when the strength of the group is built on the contributions of its members and the members derive benefits from being part of the group. Today, we are going to look at an experience of our own to explore the characteristic of interdependence. In the process, we're going to discover some other characteristics of successful groups. Our topic is, "A Time I Worked in a Successful Group."*

Think of one time when you were a part of a group that achieved something significant. The group might have been a team, or a work group with a particular task to complete. Maybe it was a family group, or a social or religious group. It might even have been a bunch of friends working together. Focus on the group's achievements. What made the group successful? What were some of the characteristics of the group that caused it to function so well? How did you feel when you were part of this group. Take a moment to think about all of these things. The topic is, "A Time I Worked in a Successful Group."

Discussion Questions:
1. How did members of the group feel toward one another?
2. What were some of the contributions that different people made to the success of the groups we discussed?
3. In what ways can groups outperform individuals?
4. Under what circumstances can individuals accomplish more alone?
5. What are some characteristics besides interdependence that make groups successful?

I Have a Friend Who Is Different From Me
A Sharing Circle

Objectives: The students will:
— identify specific differences between themselves and their friends.
— demonstrate respect for differences in race, culture, lifestyle, and ability.

Introduce the Topic: In your own words say: *Today we are going to talk about friends who are different from us and what we like about them. The topic for this session is, "I Have a Friend Who Is Different From Me."*

We are all alike in many ways, but we are also different. Today, I want you to think about a friend who is different from you in at least one major way — and tell us why you like this person so much. Perhaps your friend is of a different race, or has a much larger family, or is many years older than you. Does your friend speak a different language or eat a different way than you do? Does your friend have a disability that causes his or her lifestyle to be different from yours? Maybe your friend celebrates birthdays differently than you do, or has different holidays. Tell us what you enjoy about this person. Does your friend listen to you and share things with you? Does he or she invite you to go places? Do you have something in common like a love of sports, music, or computers? Think about it for a few minutes. The topic is, "I Have a Friend Who Is Different From Me."

Discussion Questions:
1. What are some of the ways we differ from our friends?
2. How are you enriched by the differences between you and your friend?
3. What causes people to dislike other people because of things like race or religion?
4. What would our lives be like if we could only make friends with people who are just like we are?

How I Deal with Intolerance and Prejudice
A Sharing Circle

Objectives: The students will:
—describe their reactions to acts of intolerance and prejudice.
—evaluate the effectiveness of different kinds of responses.

Introduce the Topic: In your own words say: *Our topic today is, "How I Deal with Intolerance and Prejudice." Perhaps you can think of several different ways in which you have reacted to these things. If so, just tell us about the way you respond most often. You can describe your reaction to intolerance and prejudice directed at you, or directed at someone else in your presence. Or you might decide to tell us about intolerance and prejudice that you've discovered within yourself, and how you deal with that.*

Do you get angry and challenge the other person? Do you show your disapproval with an icy stare and a cold manner? Are you assertive in expressing your opposing views? Or do you tend to ignore the person and act as if nothing happened? If you like, tell us about a specific time you responded this way, and describe how you felt. Our topic is, "How I Deal with Intolerance and Prejudice."

Discussion Questions:
1. How well does your method of dealing with prejudice and intolerance work?
2. What happens as a result of your method? Are you satisfied with the results?
3. What would happen if all the people who usually ignore intolerance started opposing it assertively?

Responsible Decision Making

Making Good Decisions
Experience Sheet and Discussion

Objectives: The students will:
—learn and practice a basic decision-making process.
—describe the importance of alternatives in decision making.
—explain how values, goals, and personal preferences affect decisions.

Materials: one copy of the experience sheet, "Decisions, Decisions!" for each student

Procedure: Distribute the experience sheets. Read through the decision-making steps listed on their experience sheets with the students, clarifying each one. Here are some ideas to discuss and questions to ask:

1. Describe the Decision to Be Made – The important first step in making a good decision is to recognize what the problem or opportunity is and clearly define it.

2. Know What is Important to You and What You Want to Accomplish – This involves such things as your likes and dislikes, values, and interests. Figuring out what's most important to you will help you make a good decision. When you know the reason why you are making a particular decision you are more likely to stick with it and follow through.

3. Gather Information - You can get information by talking to people, visiting places, watching T.V., researching on the internet, and reading. Once you have the information, you must be able to evaluate it. If two people tell you to do opposite things, how are you going to know which is right? What if neither is right?

4. List All Your Choices – By writing down your choices you will be better able to think through, and keep track of the best choices.

5. Look at Each Possible Choice and Ask Yourself What Will Happen to You and the Other People Involved if You Choose It - Look into the future.

6. Make a Decision. Decide which choice is best and make a decision - When you reach the decision point, don't freeze up. If you've done a good job on the other steps, you can choose the best alternative with confidence. Remember, if you don't choose, someone else may choose for you.

7. Develop a Plan For Putting Your Decision Into Action - Not every decision requires an action plan, but the big ones usually do. For instance, the decision to visit your grandparents in another state next summer won't come true unless you make it. And that means more decisions. Can you think what they are?

Give the students time to complete the experience sheet. As they work, circulate and offer assistance. (To allow more time, let the students complete the experience sheet as homework.)

When the students have completed their experience sheets have them choose partners. Ask them to take turns sharing the decision and decision-making process they wrote down on their experience sheets.

Lead a follow-up discussion with the entire group.

Discussion Questions

1. What did you learn about decision-making from this activity?
2. What can happen if you put off making a decision?
3. Why is it important to know your interests and values when making decisions?
4. How can having goals help you make decisions?
5. Why is it helpful to have several alternatives to choose from?
6. If you don't have alternatives, how can you develop them?
7. Why is it important to gather information when you have an important decision to make?
8. Why is it important to consider the effect your decision will have on other people?

Responsible Decision Making 153

Decisions, Decisions
Experience Sheet

The decision-making process involves <u>using what you know (or can learn) to get what you want.</u> Here are some steps to follow when you have a decision to make:

1. Describe the decision to be made.
2. Know what is important to you and what you want to accomplish.
3. Gather information. Study the information you already have. Get and study new information, too.
4. List all your choices.
5. Look at each alternative and ask yourself what will happen to you and the other people involved if you choose it.
6. Make a decision.
7. Develop a plan for putting your decision into action.

Think of a decision that you need to make. Write a description of it here:

_____
_____
_____

Now follow steps 2 through 7. Use these lines for your notes:

_____
_____
_____
_____
_____
_____
_____
_____

Thinking About Decisions

Experience Sheet and Discussion

Objectives: The students will:
—clarify personal beliefs and attitudes and how these affect decision-making.
—describe how decisions affect self and others.

Materials: one copy of the experience sheet, "Thinking About Decisions" for each student.

Procedure: Distribute the experience sheets. Review the directions with the students. Discuss the five categories for defining decisions listed on the experience sheet and give an example of each.

Have the students complete their experience sheets and then break them into small groups. Ask the students to share, within their groups, two or three of the personal decisions they have made in the past week and to discuss the reasons for their choices.

When the students have had time to share within their small groups lead a culminating discussion with the entire group.

Discussion Questions:
1. How many of your decisions were automatic?
2. Did many decisions seem out of your control?
3. What kind of decisions do you give a lot of thought to?
4. Which decisions were affected by your personal beliefs?
5. Which decisions were affected by your friends... your parents?
6. Which decisions were affected by your interests?
7. Did any of the decisions you made have an affect on other people?
8. How much did you consider the affect your decision would have on someone else before you made it?
9. When should you think about the affects of a decision – before you make it or after you make it? Explain your thinking.

Thinking About Decisions
Experience Sheet

Everyone makes decisions daily. Some decisions are more important then others. Some are so important that they require lots of thought and study before a decision is made. Others are automatic. Here are five categories for defining how decisions are made:

0 = Not under my control   **3** = I think about it but I don't study it.
1 = I do it automatically.   **4** = I study it a little bit.
2 = Sometimes I think about it.   **5** = I study it a lot.

Here is a list of decisions that someone your age might have to make. In front of each, put the number that stands for how *you would make the decision:*

_____ To get up in the morning   _____ What to eat for dinner
_____ To tell the truth   _____ To study for a test
_____ What book to read   _____ To drink alcohol
_____ To say please and thank you   _____ Who to invite to a party
_____ To look before crossing a street   _____ To go to school
_____ Where to throw trash   _____ What TV show to watch
_____ To criticize a friend behind their back   _____ What friend to hang out with on the weekend

Think back over the past week. On the lines below, describe some decisions you have made. Try to include one decision in each of these areas:
- decisions about what to do with your free time
- common, everyday decisions
- decisions about what is right and wrong
- decisions about school
- health and safety decisions

_____

_____

_____

_____

_____

What Shall We Do?
Group decision- making and discussion

Objectives: The students will:
— Make a group choice from among alternatives.
— Use communication and negotiation skills to reach a group decision.
— Demonstrate cooperative behavior in groups.
— Respect alternative points of view.

Materials: one copy of the following list of "Choices" for each group

Procedure: Have the students form small groups of four to six. Announce that the members of each group are going to work together to make a decision. In your own words, elaborate:

I want you to pretend that you are the student council for our school. This is an exciting time for you because you have an important decision to make. The council has been given $10,000 by an anonymous donor. You must decide how to spend the money. However, the donor has narrowed your range of choices. You must decide from among six alternatives.

Give each group a copy of the list of choices. Read through the list with the students.

Choices

- Take the student council (your group) to Disney World.
- Donate the money to a local children's hospital to be used to help with the treatment of a child from an uninsured family.
- Host a big party, fair, or festival for the entire school.
- Donate the money to a homeless shelter.
- Fund badly needed athletic equipment for the school.
- Put the money in a savings account for the student council.

Explain to the students that they will have 20 minutes to reach a decision. List the following rules for interaction on the board and discuss as needed:

— One person speaks at a time, with no interruptions.
— Listen to and consider the ideas and opinions of all members.
— Consider the benefits and drawbacks of each alternative.
— Agree on one choice that is acceptable to all members of the group.

After calling time, give the groups an additional 5 minutes to discuss their behavior during the decision-making process. Then ask each group to share what their decision was and how they reached it.

When all the groups have shared, conclude the activity by asking these and/or your own questions to help the students reflect on their learning.

Discussion Questions:

1. What kind of communication took place in your group?
2. What were the major disagreements in your group?
3. What did you do to resolve disagreements?
4. How easy or difficult was it for your group to come to a decision?
5. What did you learn about group decision-making?
6. In reaching your decision how much did you consider the needs of others outside your "student council" group?

Variations: Have the groups achieve consensus on a first and second choice; on first, second, and third choices; or on a rank ordering of all alternatives.

IDEAL Decision Making
Practice in Making Decisions

Objective: The students will learn and practice a simple decision making process.

Materials: the IDEAL decision making process written on the board (see below); one copy of the experience sheet "IDEAL Decision Making Steps" for each student; decision situations written on index cards or slips of paper (listed at the end of the activity)

Directions: Begin by asking the students to make some "quick decisions:"

—Would you rather have a hamburger or a hot dog?
—Would you rather go to the beach or the park?
—Would you rather watch a movie or read a book?
—Would you rather do math or history homework first?

Explain that these are examples of simple, quick decisions we all make daily.

Next, ask the students to think about, and share, some decisions they have actually made today. These might include what clothes to wear, food to eat, route to take to school, whom to hang out with, what book to read at school, etc.

Point out that the more important a decisions is, the more care and attention are required in making a final choice. Introduce and explain the IDEAL decision making process. Illustrate the process using a familiar example, such as deciding what gift to buy for a friend. Write all of your thoughts and alternatives on the board adjacent to these steps:

- **I**dentify the problem or issue to be decided.
- **D**escribe the possibilities. (What choices do you have?)
- **E**valuate your ideas. (Ask, "What could happen if I make this choice?")
- **A**ct. (Make a decision and act on it.)
- **L**earn from the decision. (Evaluate the results of the decision.)

Have the students form teams of three or four. Pass out an "IDEAL Decision Making Steps" experience sheet to each student. Briefly review the steps again and point out that by following these steps they are more likely to reach a good decision.

Give a decision card to each group. Announce that the groups have 10 minutes to make a decision, following the IDEAL process, Since the students cannot actually evaluate their decisions (final step), they should state how they would evaluate them if the situations were real.

When the students have made their decisions have each group explain their decisions to the entire class. After each report, ask several open-ended questions to stimulate discussion and help the students reflect on their learning.

Discussion Questions:

1. How did the IDEAL decision making process help you?
2. What was the hardest part about using it?
3. How well did you work together as a group?
4. Why is it important to get information when you have an important decision to make?
5. What can you do when you find that a decision isn't working?
6. What have you learned about decision making from going through this activity?

SITUATIONS:

1. You received incorrect change while shopping. *Decide what to do.*

2. Several of your friends have gotten trendy haircuts recently. You want one too, and have the money, but your parents don't like the haircuts at all. *What do you do?*

3. Your older brother wants to borrow your new T-shirt, but last time he borrowed a shirt, he returned it stained. *What do you do?*

4. You love chocolate, but frequently get a headache when you eat it. Your friend offers you a brownie with fudge frosting. *What do you do?*

5. You want to be in the band, but it would conflict with participating in sports during part of the year. *What do you do?*

6. Your friend's parents are not home. The friend gets into the liquor cabinet, opens a bottle of wine, and offers you some. *What do you do?*

7. You and a couple of friends are shopping. You see one of your friends steal a magazine. *What do you do?*

8. You invite a friend to go with you to the movies. In the afternoon, the friend calls and says they have been invited to spend the night at another friend's house. *What do you do?*

IDEAL Decision Making Steps
Experience sheet

Everyday, you make many decisions. Some are big decisions, and some are so small you don't even think of them at all. However, even with small decisions that you're not thinking about your brain goes through certain steps. But, when you're faced with a big decision you should **Think** about, and **Follow**, certain decision making steps. This will give you the best chance of making a good decision. A good way to remember what steps to follow is to learn the acronym **IDEAL**. Then you can go through these important steps anytime you're faced with a big decision.

- **I**dentify the problem or issue to be decided.

- **D**escribe the possibilities. (What choices do you have?)

- **E**valuate your ideas. (Ask, "What could happen if I make this choice?")

- **A**ct. (Make a decision and act on it.)

- **L**earn from the decision. (Evaluate the results of the decision.)

Responsibility Log
Self-Assessment

Objectives: The students will:
—explain what it means to be responsible.
—relate specific examples of responsible behavior.
—monitor and describe in writing their responsible and irresponsible behaviors for a prescribed period.

Materials: two or more copies of the experience sheet "Responsibility Log" for each student

Procedure: Begin by discussing the meaning of the word responsibility. List the following four components of responsibility on the board and ask the students to think of specific examples that might fit under each one. (Nonspecific examples are listed below in the form of do's and don'ts.) Invite the students to share incidents from their own experience.

1. Accountability
- Think before you act.
- Before you make a decision or take an action, think about how it will affect the other people involved. What will be the consequences?
- When you do something wrong or make a mistake, admit it and accept the consequences. Don't blame others or make excuses.
- Don't take credit for the achievements of others.
- Do what you should do, or have agreed to do, even if it is difficult.

2. Excellence
- Set a good example in everything you do.
- Do your best.
- Don't quit — keep trying.
- Make it your goal to always be proud of your performance (schoolwork, homework, projects, completed chores, athletic or other performances, etc.)

3. Self-control or self-restraint
- Always control yourself.
- Control your temper — don't throw things, scream, hit others or use bad language.
- Wait your turn.

- Show courtesy and good manners.

4. Being a good sport
- Win and lose with grace.
- Don't brag when you win or complain and make excuses when you lose.
- Take pride in how you play the game, not just whether you win.

Continue the discussion until the students understand the meaning of responsibility and many specific examples of responsible behavior have been shared. Then announce that, for the next few days, the students are going to keep logs describing actions that are clearly responsible and clearly not responsible.

Distribute the "Responsibility Log" and go over the directions with the students. Explain that the students should write down actions that they know are responsible (doing their best on a homework assignment and completing it on time; admitting when they forget to do a chore; congratulating the other team when they lose a game, etc.) as well as actions they feel are not responsible (not paying attention in class, blaming another person, procrastinating on an assignment, etc.).

Announce a date when the completed logs are due. Allow from 2 to 5 days, depending on the maturity of your students. Commend (for their responsibility) those students who complete the logs on time.

Before collecting the logs, have the students share their results in groups of four. Finally, lead a culminating class discussion.

Discussion Questions:

1. Which do you have more of, actions which are responsible or actions which are not responsible?
2. What surprised you about the results of your log?
3. How do you feel when you take a responsible action? How do you feel when your actions are not responsible?
4. In which area of responsibility do you think you need to improve?

Responsibility Log
Experience Sheet

For the next few days, pay close attention to your actions. Write down things you say and do that are clearly responsible actions. Also, write down things you say and do that you realize are not responsible actions.

Action	Responsible?	Reactions of Others

I Learned _____

Action	Responsible?	Reactions of Others

I Learned _____

Action	Responsible?	Reactions of Others

I Learned _____

Action	Responsible?	Reactions of Others

I Learned _____

Action	Responsible?	Reactions of Others

I Learned _____

Action	Responsible?	Reactions of Others

I Learned _____

Action	Responsible?	Reactions of Others

I Learned _____

Action	Responsible?	Reactions of Others

I Learned _____

Action	Responsible?	Reactions of Others

I Learned _____

How Would You Handle This Situation Responsibly?
Writing and Discussion

Objectives:	The students will: —describe a personal experience involving the issue of responsibility. —define ethical behavior in relation to real situations.
Materials:	writing materials
Procedure:	**Note:** This activity requires two or more class sessions. Begin the first session by asking the students to think of situations they have faced in which it was hard to choose the most responsible thing to do. For example, what do you do when you have made a commitment to participate in a meeting, and something else comes up that is equally important and more attractive to you? Or what do you do when a close friend is involved in something illegal, unethical, or dangerous? Discuss a few examples, including one from your own experience. Ask the students to write about one personal experience of this nature, without putting their names on their stories. Allow plenty of time to complete the writing in class, or assign it as homework. Collect the completed stories. Read all of the stories and select four or five to review aloud in the second class session. The best kinds of stories to select are ones that: • reflect typical binds that the students can relate to. • provide sufficiently detailed information to give the reader/listener most or all pertinent facts. Begin the second session by reading one of the stories. Emphasize that the identity of the student who wrote the story is not important. Have the class brainstorm possible ways — either responsible or irresponsible — to handle the situation described in the story. Write all suggestions on the board.

Next, discuss with the students what constitues responsible and irresponsible behavior. Explain that this will not be about the story you just read, but about behavior in general. List their ideas on the board. In this discussion be sure to refer to:

1. the rights of individuals to meet their own needs.
2. the importance of not harming others.
3. standards of honesty, integrity, and ethical behavior
4. how such values and beliefs can be reconciled when they appear to conflict.

Return to the suggestions you listed on the board for handling the situation described in the story. Ask the students which are responsible and which are not. Circle the suggestions that the students generally agree are responsible. Follow this procedure with the other stories you have selected. You may wish to spread this over several class sessions.

Conclude the activity by conducting an informal discussion asking the students to share recent personal experiences in which they consciously pondered alternatives before doing what seemed best.

Use these and your own questions to help the students reflect on their learnings.

Discussion Questions:

1. How do you resolve an ethical dilemma like the ones some of us described? What process do you use?
2. Do you tend to look at each situation individually, or do you always apply certain basic standards? Explain.
3. How do you feel when your decision violates your own ethical standards?

Practice in Problem Solving
Activity and Discussion

Objectives: The students will:
—become familiar with a problem-solving process
—generate and evaluate solutions to hypothetical and real problems

Materials: an advice column such as "Dear Abby" (current and archived Dear Abby columns are available on the internet), There are also other current on-line advise columns, several devoted to young people; 4" by 6" index cards; one copy of the experience sheet, "Problem-Solving Flow Chart", for each student.

Procedure: Bring the advice column to class. Read a typical problem to the students. Choose one that they can relate to, for example, one involving kids. Do not read the columnist's answer. Instead, ask the students: What answer would you give to this person?

Listen to the ideas of several students, clarifying and feeding back what you hear. Ask two or three of these students how they arrived at their solutions and note the steps (if any) on the board.

Distribute the index cards. Have the students each think of a typical problem that someone their age might have, and write it on the card as though writing to an advice columnist. Tell them to use the salutation, "Dear Class" and to sign a fictitious name like "Worried in the Back of the Room" or "Hiding Under My Desk." Collect all of the problem cards.

Pass out the "Problem Solving Flow Chart" to the students. Review the process depicted on the flow chart helping the students understand each problem-solving step and how the process flows. As you present the steps talk briefly about each one (suggested comments are in parentheses below).

Steps for Solving a Problem Responsibly

1. Stop all blaming. (Blaming is a waste of time and energy and does not help solve the problem.)
2. Define the problem. (Try to describe all parts of the problem. You can't solve something that you don't understand.)
3. Consider asking for help. (Some problems can't be solved alone. Would it help to talk this over with someone you trust?)

Responsible Decision Making

4. Think of possible solutions. (Think of as many as you can. You may need to get more information in order to do this.)
5. Evaluate the solutions. (Ask yourself, what will happen to me and others if I choose this one?)
6. Choose a solution. (Pick the one that has the best chance of working. It doesn't have to be perfect.)
7. Implement the solution. (This takes planning. Decide what steps to take, as well as how and when to take them.)
8. Ask yourself, Did my solution work? (Is the problem gone? If so, it worked. If not, pick a different solution and try again.)

Ask the students to keep these steps in mind as they discuss solutions to the problems you are about to read. Randomly choose one of the student generated cards and read it aloud. Act as a facilitator as the students discuss the problem and possible solutions. Guide them through the steps, when appropriate, up to and including step #6, "Choose a solution". At this point, ask the class to choose one solution to recommend. If the students are able to agree, ask someone to write the solution on the back of the card. Set the card aside.

Repeat this procedure with additional cards, as time allows. During the last few minutes of the session, lead a summary discussion.

Discussion Questions:

1. What did you learn from solving other people's problems?
2. Why is it important to define a problem correctly?
3. When do you think a kid should ask for help in solving a problem?
4. How difficult was it to come up with several possible solutions to these problems?
5. Why is it important to have choices?
6. If a solution doesn't work, what should you do?
7. Why is it important to consider how your solution could affect others?
8. How is this process like the one you use to solve your own problems? How is it different?

Problem-Solving Flow Chart
Experience Sheet

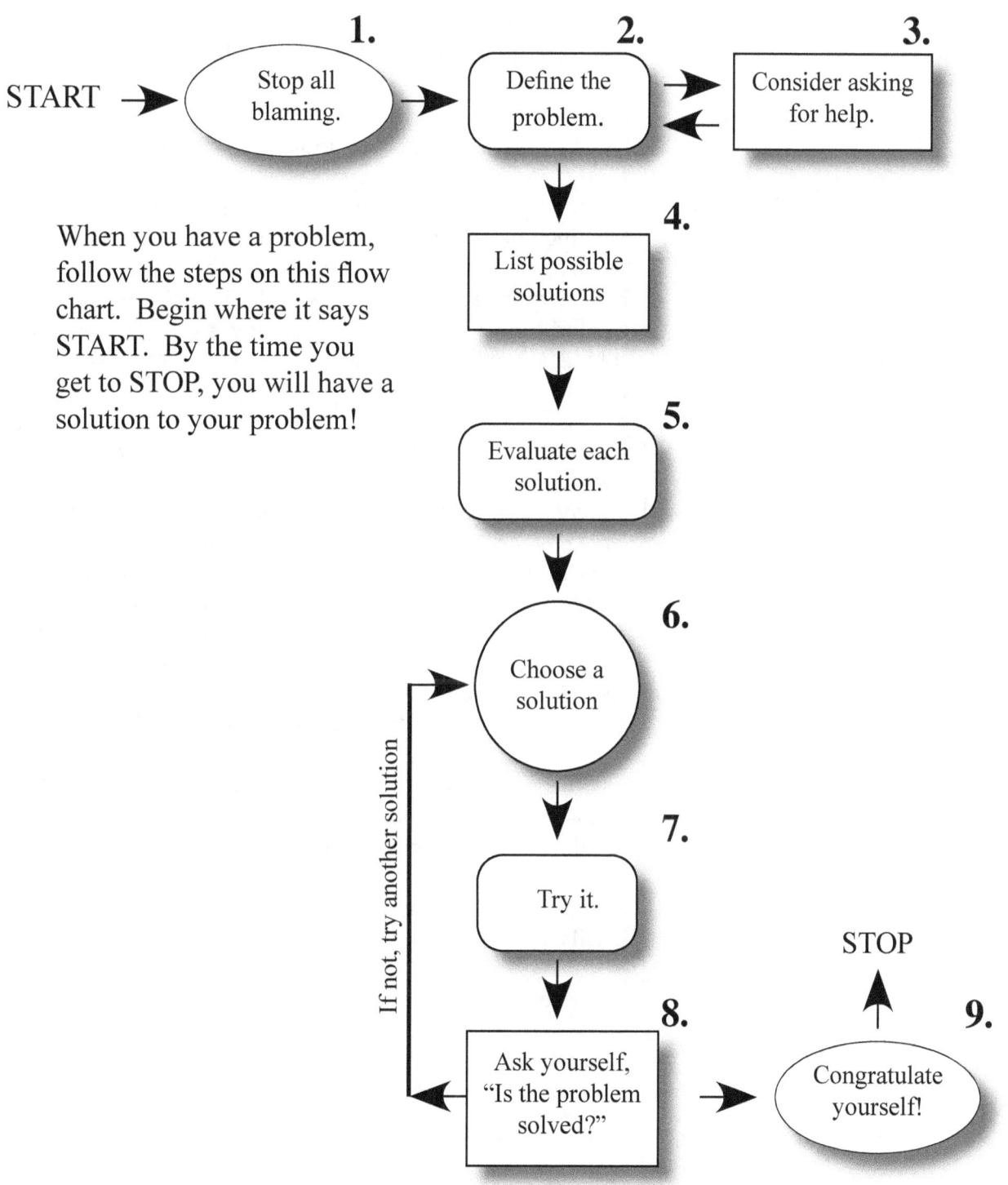

When you have a problem, follow the steps on this flow chart. Begin where it says START. By the time you get to STOP, you will have a solution to your problem!

171

What's Your Idea?
Brainstorm and discussion

Objectives: The students will:
—Experience the power of focused critical thinking.
—Understand that problems often have multiple solutions, and goals can be reached in many ways.
—Learn and apply critical thinking skills.

Materials: timer or clock/watch with a second hand; list of topics (see below) written on the board prior to the session; writing materials

Procedure: Tell the students that you want their help in doing some critical thinking. Ask the students how many know what brainstorming is. Listen to the comments of those who have participated in brainstorming sessions before and clarify that brainstorming is a process in which many ideas or solutions are generated for solving a problem or handling a situation. In your own words, explain:

Imagine that you and a friend want to surprise another friend by doing something special on his or her birthday. There are many possible things that you could do, but until you think of them you can't do them. The more ideas you come up with, the better your chances of choosing the perfect surprise. You decide to hold a brainstorming session. You spend five minutes listing as many ideas as you can think of. You write them all down and you don't stop to discuss any of them until the five minutes are up. You just keep thinking and throwing out ideas. Afterwards you go back and talk about each idea and then agree on the best one.

Ask the students if they can help you make a list of rules for brainstorming based on the process you just described. You should end up with these rules on the board:

Suggest as many ideas as you can think of. Don't worry about details, just be creative.

Write down every idea.

Don't reject, put down, evaluate, or discuss any idea during the brainstorming process.

Have the students form small groups of four or five and choose a recorder. Make sure that the recorders have paper and pencils. Then, in your own words, explain the assignment.

Pick a topic from the list on the board. I will give you the signal to start brainstorming. You will have three minutes to come up with as many ideas as you can think of. Write them all down and be sure to follow the rules. At the end of three minutes, I'll give you the signal to stop.

Circulate and observe the groups. Call time at the end of three minutes. Do a quick check of each group, commenting on the number of ideas generated and reinforcing the students for their creativity. Review any rules that the students had difficulty with.

If possible, have the groups repeat the process several more times, using new topics during each round. Do not evaluate (or allow the students to evaluate) any suggested ideas. Focus entirely on gaining practice in brainstorming. Reserve about 20 minutes for a culminating discussion.

Topics

What can you do to help out at home?
How can you surprise your mother on her birthday?
How can you make your room a better place to study?
What can you do to have fun on a rainy Saturday?
What can you do if you get lost?
What can you do if you think someone is following you?
How can we rearrange the classroom to make it better?
What kind of class party shall we have for the holidays?
How can we show our thanks as a class on Thanksgiving?
How can we make the school more attractive?
How can you meet and make new friends?
How can we decide who goes first in a game?

Discussion Questions:
1. What was easiest about brainstorming? What was hardest?
2. How did you feel and what did you do when someone suggested a wild or crazy idea?
3. Why is it important to think of many different possibilities when you are trying to solve a problem?
4. Why not just do the first thing that pops into your head?
5. Once you have a long list of ideas, what do you do next?

Current Events Research
Problem solving and discussion

Objectives: The students will:
—Summarize a current events article on an important issue or event.
—Generate solutions to a current events problem presented by the teacher.
—Generate and choose solutions to a problem.

Materials: current events articles obtained by you and the students prior to class

Procedure: Ask the students to obtain a current events article from a newspaper, news magazine, or reputable online news site. Have them bring a hard copy of the article to school on the day of the activity. Require that the articles deal with an issue or event of some importance. Bring an article of your own dealing with a problem for which creative solutions are obviously needed.

Talk to the students about the importance of being well informed. Explain that the world is shaped by the interest and participation of individuals working together to build, produce, feed, govern, and educate. In the process they create conflicts and problems that must be solved. Ask the students what kinds of issues, events, and problems they discovered while reading news articles. Ask two or three volunteers to briefly tell the class what they learned.

Have the students form pairs and take turns sharing their articles. Allow about 5 minutes for this. Then read your article aloud to the class. Define terms used in the article and discuss the problem. Ask these questions:

—What is the problem?
—Whose problem is it?

Announce that through group discussion the students are going to come up with solutions to the problem described in the article you read.

Have the students form groups of three to five. Have each group choose a leader and a recorder. Then announce that the groups

174 Responsible Decision Making

will have 20 minutes to brainstorm solutions to the problem. Review the rules for brainstorming and post them in a location visible to everyone.

Rules for Brainstorming

- Think of as many possible solutions as you can in the allotted time.
- Use your imagination and be creative.
- Do not question, criticize, or evaluate any suggestion during the brainstorming process.
- After the brainstorming period is closed, go back and evaluate and discuss the suggestions.
- As a group, agree on the best solution.

Call time after 10 minutes to close the brainstorming. Then have the groups discuss and evaluate their suggestions for 10 additional minutes. Their task is to choose one solution to present to the class. Suggest that they answer these questions:

—Will this solution solve the problem?
—Can this solution actually be done?
—Will combining any suggestions make a better solution?

Allow a few more minutes for discussion. Have the group leaders report to the class.

Culminate the activity by asking these and/or your own quesitons to help the students reflect on their learnings.

Discussion Questions:

1. What was the hardest part about finding a solution to this problem?
2. If your group was not able to come to a decision, why not?
3. How were disagreements or conflicts handled in your group?
4. How will learning to solve problems here in the classroom help prepare us to solve them in the outside world?

I Had a Hard Time Choosing Between Two Things
A Sharing Circle

Objectives:	The students will: —identify choices they have made. —explain that choosing one thing often means giving up others.
Introduce the Topic:	In your own words say: *Our topic for this session has to do with decision-making, and I'm sure all of us will be able to relate to it. Have you ever been in a situation where you were torn between two things and couldn't make up your mind? If so, you'll appreciate this topic. It is, "I Had a Hard Time Choosing Between Two Things."* *Tell us about a time when you had to choose one thing over another because we couldn't have both. Maybe you wanted to go to two different places at the same time, or you wanted to buy two things and only had enough money for one. Or describe some other type of situation in which you had to choose between two different things. Think about it for a few moments. The topic is, "I Had a Hard Time Choosing Between Two Things."*
Discussion Questions:	1. How did you feel about giving up the thing you didn't choose? 2. How is making a decision the same thing as taking a risk? 3. Someone once said that after you make your decision, you need to move out of "what if" and move into "it is," What does that mean? 4. Is the best choice for one person the best choice for everyone? Why?

I Made a Decision Based on the Facts
A Sharing Circle

Objectives: The students will:
—recognize the importance of making fair decisions
—describe how weighing facts and evidence contributes to making fair decisions.

Introduce the Topic: In your own words say: *Our topic for this session is, "I Made a Decision Based on the Facts." Have you ever been in a situation where you had to decide something, and you wanted to be very fair? If you have, then you probably realize that to be fair you have to set aside your own feelings and try to look at facts and information. For instance, maybe you were asked to help choose a new team member for soccer or Little League. You couldn't simply choose the person you liked best; you had to choose the best player. Perhaps you had to decide the winner in some kind of contest. Instead of giving the prize to your best friend, you awarded it to the person who did the best job. Or maybe you had to help settle an argument between two younger children. To make a fair decision, you needed to hear both sides and gather as much information as you could. We all have many opportunities to make fair decisions. Tell us about one that you made. Take a few moments to think about it. The topic is, "I Made a Decision Based on the Facts."*

Discussion Questions:
1. How did you feel when you were making a decision in the situation you shared?
2. What makes a decision fair?
3. Why do people make decisions without looking at the facts?
4. If you have to make a decision and don't have enough information, what can you do?

A Time I Stood Up for Something I Strongly Believe In
A Sharing Circle

Objectives: The students will:
—describe and take credit for situations in which they demonstrated the courage of their convictions.
—describe what it feels like to take an unpopular public position.

Introduce the Topic: In your own words say: *Today's topic is, "A Time I Stood Up for Something I Strongly Believe In." Most of us have probably experienced at least once the necessity to take a stand concerning something. Standing up for a belief can be difficult, especially if friends or relatives do not agree with us. Even when they do agree, it is not necessarily easy to state our beliefs publicly. Think of a time when this happened to you.*

Maybe you saw others doing something that you felt was wrong, and you confronted them. Perhaps you were involved in a discussion about a controversial subject, and you stated your views, even though they were unpopular. You may remember being nervous and worrying about the uncertainty of the situation. Or you may have felt very sure of yourself. Perhaps when you look back on the occasion, you recall a sense of pride, accomplishment, or even daring. If the outcome was different from what you wanted, tell us what you learned from the experience. Remember, don't mention any names. The topic is, "A Time I Stood Up for Something I Strongly Believe In."

Discussion Questions:
1. What similarities were there in our reasons for standing up for what we believe in?
2. When is it hardest for you to stand up for your beliefs?
3. What conditions enable you to stand up for what you believe in?

A Responsible Habit I've Developed
A Sharing Circle

Objectives: The students will:
—describe and take credit for responsible behaviors.
—realize that responsible habits are developed through repeated practice.

Introduce the Topic: In your own words say: *No matter how responsible we already are, we can always learn more about this important value. It's also important to give ourselves credit for the responsible things we do on a regular basis. Our topic for this sharing circle is, "A Responsible Habit I've Developed."*

When we do something again and again it becomes a habit. That's how some of our responsible actions become habits. We do them so often we don't even think about them anymore. Do you have any habits like that? Maybe you brush your teeth every day without being reminded, put your dirty clothes in a hamper as soon as you take them off, or pick up things you see lying around the house. Perhaps you feed and exercise a pet regularly, make your bed as soon as you get up in the morning, or check every weekend to see if you can do anything to assist an elderly neighbor. Or maybe you always finish your homework before watching TV, or your yard chores before going off with friends on Saturday. Think it over and tell us about a responsible action that you do regularly. Our topic is, "A Responsible Habit I've Developed."

Discussion Questions:
1. How does having a responsible habit make you feel about yourself?
2. Can you simply decide to develop a habit and then do it? Why or why not?
3. How are habits developed?
4. What responsible habits did you hear about today that you would like to develop, too?

How I Helped a Friend Solve a Problem
A Sharing Circle

Objective: The students will describe ways in which working together can overcome problems.

Introduce the Topic: In your own words say: *When it comes to solving problems, sometimes two heads are better than one. We're going to talk about times like this in today's circle. The topic is, "How I Helped a Friend Solve a Problem".*

We all get into a jam from time to time and need the help of others. Think of a time when you helped a friend solve a problem that they couldn't solve alone. Perhaps your friend wanted to go on a bike ride with another friend but he didn't have a bike, so you lent him yours for the day. Maybe your class got a new student who didn't know anyone, so you went out of your way to be friendly and introduced her to others in the class. Have you ever had friends who were angry at each other and had a fight, and you helped them make up. Perhaps you helped a friend find her lost dog. There are many ways we can help others. Think of a time you helped a friend who had a problem. Tell us how you helped and what kinds of feelings you had in the situation? The topic is, "How I Helped a Friend Solve a Problem".

Discussion Questions:
1. Why do we need to work together to solve problems?
2. How do you feel when you have helped someone solve a problem?
3. How does everyone benefit when someone helps someone else solve a problem?

How My Decision Affected Someone Else
A Sharing Circle

Objective: The students will describe how decisions affect self and others

Introduce the Topic: In your own words say: *Our topic for today is, "How My Decision Affected Someone Else." Have you ever made a decision and been aware that someone else was either helped or hurt by it? Maybe you made a new friend and decided to spend time with them every chance you got. How did this decision affect your new friend? How did it affect your old friends? Maybe you decided to go camping instead of to soccer practice. How did that decision affect other members of the team? Other people are affected by the things we do and also by the things we say. Doing things like being polite, being friendly, and telling the truth affects others. But being impolite, unfriendly and telling lies also affects others. Tell us about a decision you made, but concentrate on describing the affect your decision had on others. When you are ready to share the topic is, "How My Decision Affected Someone Else."*

Discussion Questions:
1. Why is it that so many of our decisions affect others?
2. Can you think of any types of decisions that don't affect others?
3. Why should you think about the affects of a decision before you take action on the decision?

Responsible Decision Making